I read everything Kenny Luck writes! Why? Because he knows the heart of men and writes to us in a straightforward manner. I read his words and think, *How does he know me so well?* In *Failsafe*, you will find yourself nodding along, and then you'll be challenged deeply to look past your need for approval or fear of failure to God's love as the ultimate failsafe. Read this and live with the security that your soul craves. I highly recommend.

DOUG FIELDS, speaker, pastor, author of *7 Ways to Be Her Hero*

QRF (Quick Reaction Force). No operation ever goes exactly as planned on the battlefield. Should things take a turn for the worse, a radio transmission to the QRF will get help on the way. In *Failsafe*, Kenny Luck explores how God's love is a man's ever-present QRF, providing us with cover fire, air support, armor, tactical proficiency, and intel that falls from heaven. God's special forces take ground and victory when the failsafe is in place.

CHAD WILLIAMS, former Navy SEAL, author of *SEAL of God*

If you want to understand what it really means to embrace God's acceptance and then be freed to love other people as a result, *Failsafe* is a game changer. I couldn't recommend this book more highly, and I'm grateful Kenny wrote it. Just be careful—there's a good chance it will convict you and push you out of your comfort zone. But isn't that what it takes to be the kind of man God wants you to be? I hope you're up for the challenge.

SEAN MCDOWELL, PhD, Biola University professor, speaker, author

SEAL teams always have a Plan A, B, C, and D. Why? Because things rarely go as planned. *Failsafe* explores our backup plan as Christian men, that one special place that never fails and is always safe: the loving arms of God. As believers, when we stumble or fail, we are caught by God's unfailing security. It is also our base from which we pick ourselves up and move forward. Kenny Luck is the real deal, and he speaks out of a walk with God that carried him through many difficult moments. *Failsafe* is a must-read for every man who wishes to stay on mission.

MILAN YERKOVICH, author of *How We Love*, founder of Relationship 180

Kenny
Luck

Failsafe

Living Secure in God's Acceptance

A NavPress resource published in alliance
with Tyndale House Publishers

NavPress is the publishing ministry of The Navigators, an international Christian organization and leader in personal spiritual development. NavPress is committed to helping people grow spiritually and enjoy lives of meaning and hope through personal and group resources that are biblically rooted, culturally relevant, and highly practical.

For more information, visit NavPress.com.

CONTENTS

You should never live according to what you lack.

NICK VUJICIC,
LIFE WITHOUT LIMITS

INTRODUCTION

The Inner Man

I TEACH A CLASS at my church for prospective members. It's what you might expect—an orientation to the history of our church, our present direction, our biblical views, and our vision for the future. People who attend the class have already taken a test-drive of our services and checked out our kids' programs. Most have prayed about becoming members, and their presence is a sign they're ready for that step. About midway through the class, we reach a section in the materials that speaks to the kind of faith community we're seeking to build. Some themes in this section, for example, include a "worshiping" community and a "joy-filled" community. And then we reach this theme: "*a masculine-friendly community.*" In most churches, men aren't a signature part of the vision for the community they're building, but this is a functional and practical distinctive of our church that receives a lot of staff time, attention, and investment.

This moment is a gut check for most people in the class.

I can see both the look and the temperature in the room change. The faces of most of the women contort in some way, eyebrows furrow, arms fold, and bodies shift in chairs. I understand where the discomfort comes from in a culture where people don't see much to celebrate in men. Who could blame them? They see headline after headline of men acting in their own self-interests at the expense of others. Names might be popping into your mind right now from headlines on cable news. The common denominator? Men who have used their influence, position, or power to abuse others. Think sexual-abuse scandals. Think mass killings. Think human trafficking. Think domestic violence. Think fatherlessness. Think of all the chaos and dysfunction that flow from the choices grown men make out of boy-sized emotional maturity and character. It's head-scratching and confirms the fact that age, skill, high achievement, wealth, discipline, and unbroken successes have *nothing* to do with a man's *emotional* maturity. So when I announce to a roomful of potential members that our church is building a community of masculine-friendly Christ followers, it seems like an oxymoron to many. It's confusing and lacking in context.

Behind the discomfort, the obvious intrigue, the furrowed eyebrows, the folded arms, and the bodies shifting in seats is a simple thought: *Why would a church want to empower existing broken male culture?* But before numerous mental rabbit trails are taken, I quickly preempt the mystery with a cascade of answers, starting with this:

> Our church believes that one of the greatest gifts we can give our community, our women, and our children is a spiritually healthy, relationally committed, and emotionally grown-up man.

The word choice here is specific and intentional. It resonates at a deep level with both men and women because everyone understands the very real consequences connected to a twelve-year-old twenty-year-old, a thirteen-year-old thirty-year-old, a fourteen-year-old forty-year-old, and so on. Everyone knows that boy-sized emotional maturity and character in a man-sized body with man-sized commitments and responsibilities spells D-I-S-A-S-T-E-R. That's why the world hopes (just as our church does) that we as men will grow up and out of the boy on the inside into mature men who can say no to ourselves and our lesser impulses in order to say yes to loving God and others well. In other words, our church wants to make sure that our women and children have mature servant-leaders as husbands, fathers, friends, and neighbors. But more importantly, our church wants men to know that we don't buy the narrative peddled in culture that men are somehow the failed brand that can't be trusted with the important relationships, partnerships, and decisions of life.

We're saying to our people and our community that masculine strength is not just a good thing, but it's a great thing when equally strong emotional maturity, character, and compassion are guiding it. We want our women to know that we have their backs, and we understand the pain this broken male culture inflicts on women and children for generations. We want to create a space where men become healthy and strong in all the right ways, because being the right kind of man for others is one of God's most powerful and richest blessings.

Becoming that blessing is a war for the masculine soul.

Little Boys and Grown Men

I laugh about it *now*.

My fourth-grade class picture in elementary school tells the whole story—from the inside out. It's a classic shot. Four evenly packed rows of elementary-aged boys and girls across metal bleachers, our faces innocent and our countenances unspoiled by the self-consciousness of the social media age. Envision simple plaid shirts, girls with pigtails, precious smiles, and perfectly still little spirits staring intently into the camera.

"Say cheese!" *Click.*

Today we snap six or seven pictures on a smartphone in five seconds, select the best one in the next ten seconds, and then text it to friends or post it to social media in the following thirty seconds. But in the 1970s, school photographers couldn't pre-inspect a photo. For perspective, the advent of mainstream digital cameras was two decades away. Instead, photographers had to wait until the film was professionally developed directly from negatives in a darkroom, and then dried and cut before seeing whether their vision was realized. A fast turnaround was *days*.

On this particular fall day, the photographer assigned to John Muir Elementary must have been weary, in a hurry, apathetic, or all of the above, because Miss Casey's fourth-grade class was a one-click-and-done deal. Our photographer didn't think to take a backup picture. But then again, most children were able to hold off poking one another and stand at attention for the time it took a single-lens reflex camera shutter to open and close, right? What could go wrong?

That class-picture experience faded quickly out of my memory, because there was no purpose in thinking about it again until the ever-exciting last week of school, when the Wildcat yearbook was passed out to the entire school. That was the week of the school year when we watched a lot of films, had a lot of class parties, and were handed a yearbook to reminisce over and sign.

With my yearbook in hand, I had only one mission: to find pictures of myself! Drawing mustaches and beards on my least favorite teachers' faces could wait for a lazy summer day.

I tore into my copy, scanning the pages, scrutinizing the pictures, and trying to spot myself playing prison ball, kickball, tetherball, or any other "ball." I was disappointed to find only a few candid shots of myself in the fourth-grade section. The boring catharsis of looking at your yearbook at this age is the class picture, of course—no playground, no ball, no action shots there, right?

Wrong.

When I turned the page to Miss Casey's fourth-grade class, there was some action, and unfortunately, it would be forever memorialized in time. Four even rows of children? Check. Girls with pigtails? Check. Precious smiles? Check. Perfectly still children staring intently into the camera? *All but one.*

My head was turned sideways, perfectly perpendicular to the camera lens, and it was obvious I was trying to get the attention of the boy next to me, my open mouth three inches from his right ear. True to form, Mr. Diarrhea Mouth (as my third-grade teacher dubbed me in my report card the previous year) was behaving in an untimely and unwelcome way, ruining this otherwise pristine fourth-grade moment in time.

The adage "A picture is worth a thousand words" is painfully real to me looking at this image after all these years, but it's also very humanizing. Clearly, my behavior captured in this freeze-frame suggests a need to talk, a need to connect, a need to receive some kind of feedback, and a need to be acknowledged—needs that *outweigh* the need for manners or consideration of others. I was completely unaware of what my physical context was calling for because my anxious soul was seeking worth and attention—and risking future embarrassment to get some. My thought process, in hindsight, was simple:

- If people listen to me, they see and notice me.
- If they see and notice me, I am worth something.
- If I am worth something, I matter, and that calms my fears.
- If my fears are calmed and I have peace inside, I will feel more secure and comforted.

The problem with this kind of reasoning is when we become grown men with little-boy fears still lurking inside.

Worth Is Better Than a Thousand Pictures

This yearbook picture—unlike the billions of pictures we pose for and display in our social media feeds today—reveals the unvarnished truth about my *inner* formation as an adolescent and a young adult. In this picture, my insides were literally making their way outside and were *unconsciously* projected into my social matrix. That picture represents my hidden need to know something every human being seeks at a deep, fundamental level. You and I want to know . . .

- Am I worth someone's time and attention?
- Does anyone see and value me?
- Will someone accept, know, and appreciate me?

After two decades of working with men of all ages as a mental-health worker and pastor, I've found that my story is not uncommon. As the youngest of seven kids living in a chaotic home with an alcoholic parent, I could easily get lost in the shuffle of a large family ecosystem. I saw, sensed, and was immersed in constant conflict, but no one was able to help me filter what was happening—except my black Labrador. I would call Bub (the dog) to my room, instinctively petting and talking to him to distract and comfort myself in the midst of the yelling, name-calling, and door-slamming just outside my closed door. I would do this until the chaos stopped, and then I'd slowly pop my head out of my room, listening and looking for signs that all parties had returned to their respective corners. Thank God for my dog!

This was my normal.

No one talked to me. Strangely, and yet like many children do, I thought something was wrong with me—that I wasn't worth talking to. I was losing the one thing that keeps human beings hopeful: the idea that I mattered. As a result, my peace was hijacked and replaced with anxiety over possibly being the "accidental" seventh child. Or worse, a mistake. Being five years removed from my closest sibling didn't help. It was as if I was there *but not there*, because everyone else was running out of the house, running away from the house, or locking the doors to their rooms.

Fast-forward twenty-five years to a session with a counselor who asked me to pick a word from a list that best described my growing-up years. As I scanned the sheet, I saw both negative and positive words, but I found my eyes gravitating toward only one word. I then started tapping that same word in silence with my index finger.

The word was *ignored*.

I went on to tell the counselor that from a very early age, I had nervous energy driven by what I felt I lacked—basic worth—and I was living out of that. Predictably and inexorably, I took all the traditional routes young men take to validate themselves and diminish the insecurity that accompanies that awful self-perception.

I became an expert at reading social situations and changing colors like a chameleon, morphing into whatever I thought was necessary to be accepted. I simply studied the playground, saw who was getting the attention and which behaviors got it, and then pulled off those behaviors better than the next guy. Sadly, that is what deprivation of the soul will create—a young man who will do whatever it takes to be tossed some crumbs of social intimacy. The fourth-grade snapshot of me talking during the class photo sat comfortably next to my senior-class hall-of-fame picture: "Kenny Luck—Life of the Party." New picture of me, mouth open, still seeking attention, building a reputation—and wearing a mask to hide my lack of self-worth.

I was growing into an insecure man.

Authentic versus Synthetic Worth

Like a heat-seeking air-to-air missile that flies directly toward the engine of an airborne target, the human soul is engineered to seek out, locate, and secure worth. God hard-wired us to be seen, known, and appreciated by *someone*. And if someone doesn't stop, take notice, and acknowledge us in a meaningful way, our souls won't be at peace. This gap in the soul will be a conscious or subconscious force in our lives. A force that fuels fear and insecurity within.

We are never quite at peace. We're restless. We're driven. We worry too much about what others think of us. We compete to be visible. We sabotage our own relationships. We fear rejection. We protect our image. We overinvest emotionally. We hate being alone. We crave approval but have a hard time accepting it. We like order and predictability. We like control. We *don't* like surprises. We define ourselves by what other people think. We posture, trying to act tough because we're truly afraid people will discover who we really are. We publicly smile while we privately struggle with besetting temptations and struggles. We label and judge others. We get jealous in relationships.

Why? We lack deep and lasting peace on the inside.

None of what I just mentioned is God's desire or plan. His plan and desire are that all men, women, and children receive lasting peace by discovering *authentic worth* in their souls.

The key word? *Authentic*.

When it comes to our souls and their organic need to feel worth, a single, powerful truth will help us begin a new, authentic, and God-empowered experience in our inner man: *Things outside us cannot resolve the dilemmas within us.*

No relationship. No improved circumstances. No "if only" scenario. No professional title, award, or achievement. No amount of money. No amount of social visibility. No risky or new thrill. No extended absence of adversity. No amount of power or control over others. No resolution of party politics. No cosmetic fix, new look, or wardrobe. No vanquishing of obstacles. No wonder drug. No family catharsis. No religious behavior. No loosening of moral boundaries. No change of scenery. No new technology or gadget. No getaway or vacation. Not even a new black Labrador puppy.

The logic is that somehow, by a mystical osmosis, the right outer structure of our lives will create an inner order for our souls. We are hoping and wishing and behaving as if it were so, but it's not! And still, millions of people are spending billions of hours and trillions of dollars hoping that this formula for their deprived souls will work. Fostering this hope and exploiting this deep need of our souls is a dark individual who desperately wants us to continue believing that a betterment or rearrangement of things outside us will heal the wounds or deficits of character within us.

Meet the king of fear and pride: Satan.

The master counterfeiter of all things God, he is in a sophisticated recruiting war with God for control of the human soul. But since he can't deliver permanent, authentic worth to the soul, he has custom-engineered a kaleidoscope of synthetic ways for men to feel temporary forms of acceptance. These soul-teasing pursuits and counterfeits anesthetize the pain connected to a lack of worth or prop up a pseudosignificance in us while never being able to actually fill the void. They're evil prescriptions packaged and sold as popular opinions and prevailing cultural norms around the globe. In fact, that is Satan's shibboleth: *it's just culture.* These false fountains of earthly worth demand conformity and rob our best energies from our best days and God's highest intentions.

Our need for worth gets exploited, and we take the bait.

These ways of solving the soul problem are rooted in powerful "isms" or philosophies that, *if believed*, will lead to behaviors that distance a man from God. Think hedonism, materialism, and narcissism—finding worth in self-gratification, financial self-preservation, and self-importance. These were the same "isms" and expressions of identity and masculinity that Satan tempted Jesus with in the Gospels: placing his worth in these earthly things *over and above* his identity as the Son of God. Satan is keenly aware that the more we embrace them as our sources of worth, the more self-absorbed we become. As a consequence, our relationships with God and people will inevitably fragment, then atomize, and eventually dissolve.

Two words come to mind: *evil* and *effective*.

The prevalence and power of these "isms" and their multiplied expressions in broken male culture are so pervasive that, over the centuries, men have tried to blend these belief systems with faith in Christ. *It can't be done.* Not because I say it can't, but because Jesus himself did. He declared to his disciples, "You do not belong to the world."[1] This is a warning inside a declaration. We belong to him, and because of that, Jesus warns us not to blend eternal worth with forms of earthly worth. In the crudest analysis, Jesus is essentially saying, *"Don't let the culture pimp you, rip you off, or deceive you into trying to blend your worth from me with worth from the world."* Why is Christ so emphatic?

These concepts of worth are synthetic and sponsored by the hater of your soul.

This high-pressure ecosystem of broken male culture is continuously spinning beliefs, behaviors, and identities toward us through every possible medium. More importantly, they are directed intentionally toward the emptiness in our hearts that God alone can fill. As philosopher Blaise Pascal wrote in *Pensées*, "[Man] tries in vain to fill [this emptiness] with everything around him. . . . [But] this infinite abyss can be filled only with an infinite and immutable object; in other words by God himself."[2] That is why they're so powerful and deeply attractive to us, but they also fail to satisfy us deeply, because only God himself can fill that vacuum.

Synthetic, by definition, means something created to imitate the original. The call to this generation of Christ-following men is this: *Accept no imitations*. What all men seek and need is the deep, lasting, and transforming worth that comes from one source: God's love. It's that simple, but at the same time, this truest truth is powerfully attacked, opposed, muted, discredited, and polluted by an enemy who fears the power of our souls fully connecting to God's love.

This is the journey of the inner man, the fight of the masculine soul.

Locking Down Your Inner Man

There is a hidden you that the Bible calls your "inner man."[3] It's the you no one sees who . . .

- Is afraid of failing again
- Doesn't want to let others down
- Wants to be appreciated uniquely
- Isn't sure you have what it takes spiritually
- Is fighting sin alone
- Doubts God under adverse circumstances
- Struggles to tell the truth
- Compares yourself to others
- Fears what others think
- Often feels that God has deserted you

- Wonders why God isn't giving you what you need
- Is overly protective of your image
- Lets circumstances define your worth
- Is anxious about the future all the time
- Is a perfectionist, believing that your failures are fatal and final
- Has trouble receiving God's forgiveness
- Relies on yourself apart from God to solve things
- _____ (fill in the blank)

The endgame of God is to pour out his love to this *inner man*—the one that you alone know. Why? Because the critical battles are fought within your spirit, and that's where you need God most. Helping you experience victory inside and enjoy the fullness of that process is the goal of this book. It's also the hater's worst nightmare.

Listen closely to this prayer over you, which comes straight from the Spirit of God:

> I bow my knees before the Father, from whom every family in heaven and on earth derives its name, that He would grant you, according to the riches of His glory, to be strengthened with power through His Spirit in the inner man, so that Christ may dwell in your hearts through faith; and that you, being rooted and grounded in love, may be able to comprehend with all the saints what is the breadth and length and height and depth, and to know the love of Christ which surpasses knowledge, that you may be filled up to all the fullness of God.[4]

Strengthened. Rooted. Grounded. Filled up. Fully empowered. This is a picture of emotional, psychological, and spiritual security invading, overwhelming, and transforming the soul of a man.

The power of the gospel is the ability of God's love to transform the inner man—the real you—from the inside out. In the midst of your inner motives, fears, affections, concerns, and doubts, God's love is fully able to hold you upright in the changes and challenges, trials and temptations, successes and failures of life. It sustains us under pressure. It tells us who we are and who we are not. It tells us why we're alive. It tells us what to do in the moment. It tells us the truest truths about ourselves. It is soul piercing. It is pervasive. It heals the fractures. It binds our wounds. It sings over us.

> The LORD your God is with you,
>   the Mighty Warrior who saves.
> He will take great delight in you;
>   in his love he will no longer rebuke you,
>   but will rejoice over you with singing.[5]

God takes great delight in *you*! That's his mission. For some of us, that sounds so foreign. For others, we have heard it but not internalized it, so it's easy to let that truth blow past our hearts. As we journey forward into this truest truth, I will state and restate it until the walls of our hearts crumble and we become vulnerable. God's love for us is a *failsafe* when past traumas, unplanned circumstances, unhealthy self-perceptions, unwelcome rejections, and unmet expectations threaten the security of our souls. His love kicks in to save us from the slippery slopes of paralyzing anxiety, uncontrollable anger, and prolonged or systemic sadness. It is our backup when our own resources break down. God's never-failing love is *there* for us when life, our humanity, or both conspire to break us down and tempt us to give up.

You might be thinking, *But I know that already.*

Do you?

Hundreds of millions of men know in their heads that God loves them and has created them to serve him, but they fail to connect the reality of his personal love for them to the real emotions and events of their daily existence. In their minds (and perhaps in your mind), God's love is an abstract and distant spiritual truth that becomes relevant only in certain settings. This attitude and approach to God's love lead to blending the ways of culture with faith and pursuing solutions that fail to penetrate the soul. Predictably, expectations related to God go unmet, and men are left worried, disappointed, and confused about God and his love for them.

So what is happening?

God's love is in our heads, but it's not in our hearts. Most importantly, our lack of peace tells the story. Jesus says of such men, "These people honor me with their lips, but their hearts are far from me."[6]

That is why God has placed this book in your hands. He wants to clear up your confusion and usher in a fresh encounter with him. You may be encouraged to know that God is moving in his men all over the world at this moment in history and is reshaping their hearts. A movement is being born that only men secure in his love can advance. He is transitioning his beloved sons from the anxiety, emptiness, and self-loathing of securing our worth in cultural ways to a new pattern of integrating his love into the fabric of our thinking and self-perceptions. Men by the millions are internalizing, receiving, and actively comprehending "the breadth and length and height and depth" of God's love, and they are coming to "know [that] love . . . which surpasses knowledge." Because of a gracious quickening of God's Spirit, the love of God is traveling like a raging river from the heads of men downward, cascading forcefully into the deep crevasses and cavities of their hearts and securing victory for them in their inner man.

The result? *Power.*

Men healed and freed by God's love are fearless in the face of adversity and humble in the face of prosperity. *How does that work?* you ask. Because they know that God's loving purposes are being worked out in both sets of circumstances. Living in and under God's redemptive love is a mentality that sounds a lot like this:

> If God is for us, who can be against us? He who did not spare his own Son, but gave him up for us all—how will he not also, along with him, graciously give us all things? Who will bring any charge against those whom God has chosen? It is God who justifies. Who then is the one who condemns? No one. Christ Jesus who died—more than that, who was raised to life—is at the right hand of God and is also interceding for us. Who shall separate us from the love of Christ? Shall trouble or hardship or persecution or famine or nakedness or danger or sword? As it is written:

> "For your sake we face death all day long;
>   we are considered as sheep to be slaughtered."

> No, in all these things we are more than conquerors through him who loved us.[7]

Did you hear it? By accessing God's love for them in the real-time battles of life, sons of the King conquer the very things that attack their worth, seek to rob their peace, and dilute their faith. They know they will always and forever be beloved sons, fully empowered and authorized family members who possess a love and inheritance that are unbreakable. Circumstances may assail their bodies, but they don't control their spirits or assign their worth. Their sovereign Creator has assigned their worth.

How do these men live? Instead of being conquered by their fears and insecurities, they defeat them inwardly. The personal, sacrificial initiative of God through Christ has overrun and taken back inner territories previously held by fear or pride. These men have internalized and activated their worth from God emotionally, cognitively, and psychologically through the Holy Spirit. They are *living* meaningfully in God's love and are *comforted* deeply, which significantly changes every aspect of their lives.

The love of Christ controls us.[8]

[Jesus said,] "As the Father has loved me, so have I loved you. Now remain in my love."[9]

It's time for every man to make the transition. Are you ready?

Father in heaven,

I am ready for a deeper encounter with your love. I am ready for your love to take over how I view myself, my past, my present, and my future. I am ready to give you the fullest access to my inner man so that any fear—known or unknown—can be defeated and replaced by your powerful love for me. I am ready to work out in my everyday life the love you have poured into my heart through Christ. Leave no area of my life untouched by your love. I want to grasp every dimension of it so that every purpose you have for me will be fulfilled. Begin the process now, Father, of breaking down my defenses, my pride, and my fears so that the inner man—the real me—can receive your power. With all faith, hope, and eager anticipation, I pray. Amen.

GETTING SECURE

THE FIGHT IS OVER

I Am Fully Accepted

ANOTHER PARTY. A little buzzed. Alone.

I wondered what people would think if they could see what I was really thinking and feeling in this moment. I had just put on another Academy Award–winning performance as the "fun" guy telling jokes, gathering people around drinking games, and even shocking myself as to the lengths I would go to be visible and stand out.

"For what?" I lamented. This wasn't working.

More to the point, it was all coming to a head—I could literally feel it in my body. I was empty and dead inside when everyone else around me thought I was so full and alive. I was winning the battle of images but losing the battle of life. For four solid years,

I'd been chasing "cool"—that elusive, ever-changing, temporary salve for the soul that men have been substituting for God's perfect and unconditional love for centuries. Every day was a fight to put myself "out there," to win acceptance by performing in every social, athletic, academic, and interpersonal setting, and at all times, to impress everyone and win their approval. But this particular night was the equivalent of driving into a cul-de-sac of the soul. My futile quest was timing out.

What was I doing wrong?

The fight to prove myself seemed to be hitting on all cylinders. The things I thought would satisfy my inner thirst, I already possessed. Money? Check. I had three jobs and wanted for nothing at the time. Path forward? Check. I was headed to one of the best universities in the world. Social capital? Check. I was very visible, and people generally liked me. (This was before social media came on the scene.) Girlfriend? Check. She was a wonderful gal. Religious? Check. I was a regular church attender and worked at it.

So why the void?

My expectation was that somewhere along this journey, there would be a catharsis, a moment of peace, where I'd sit on the summit, take a deep breath, and bask in the satisfaction that I had secured acceptance and meaning. But it hit me that night: the reality that people tire of clapping for you, their attention is fleeting, and they are naturally into themselves. This realization pushed the summit of acceptance further away when it seemed so close. Like me, the very people I was trying to impress were thinking about their own needs and issues and were competing for the same limited resources I was competing for out there in the cruel world.

When the applause fades, and you're confronted with the reality that you are no closer to the summit than when you started, it leads to depression and gives birth to despair. It's what happens when hope-filled energy and expectations have been invested without the insight that you've been engaged in a lost cause from the very beginning. That reality can feel fatal and final.

Thankfully my despair turned to desperation.

As in most things, my motive for praying was to get God to "follow" and "like" me, too. It was part of my formula for getting to the summit of acceptance. So that summer night, like muscle memory, I started the words of my prayer as I had for years: "Our Father, who art in heaven . . ." And as I'd experienced for years, my head was disconnected from my heart as the words filed out of my mouth on autopilot. But then, surprising myself, I stopped praying.

Enter the desperation.

Like a balled-up fist exploding out of nowhere to knock someone to the ground, my heart cried out. The next sentence that burst forth from my mouth was not "hallowed be your name" but "Jesus, if you're real, I need to see you."

In a do-or-die tone, this first salvo of my prayer exchange with God had been put out there. What now? Feeling exposed and vulnerable before God himself, I doubled down and followed with a second desperate blow aimed at his mysterious and eternal chest: "Jesus, I want to see you." I repeated this multiple times as energetically, honestly, and intentionally as possible . . . until *it happened.* I secured the response I was looking for! Later on, I found this is what God promises to do when desperation and authenticity combine to project sincerity of heart.

> "You will call on me and come and pray to me, and I
> will listen to you. You will seek me and find me when
> you seek me with all your heart. I will be found by you,"
> declares the LORD.[1]

So what exactly happens when God comes into your bedroom? The short answer is that he brings his person, his presence, and his power to you. That's the normal process when you call out, and someone comes to the place where you are, right? Jesus came into the back room at the end of the hall—I felt his presence all around me and pervading my body from the inside out. I had asked to "see" him, and my heart was seeing him as clearly as if a physical body had been in front of me. More importantly, *he was seeing me as well*—my heart, my desperation, my desire for acceptance, every hope, every fear, every doubt, perfectly and all at once. The feeling of being fully seen was followed by a feeling of being fully accepted, without conditions. I was literally—physically and psychologically—sensing what I had been searching for my whole life: *to know I was okay*. I had reached the summit, but I didn't have to climb any more mountains, impress any more people, humiliate myself, or become anyone other than me for Jesus to fully accept me. I was being healed by a power encounter with the real and risen Christ. That single experience is as mysterious and personal as it gets. But Christ was straightforward.

He said, "*The fight is over for you, Kenny.*"

God, who knows the heart, showed that he accepted
[the Gentiles] by giving the Holy Spirit to them,
just as he did to us. He did not discriminate between
us and them, for he purified their hearts by faith.
Now then, why do you try to test God by putting
on the necks of Gentiles a yoke that neither we nor
our ancestors have been able to bear? No! We believe
it is through the grace of our Lord Jesus that we are
saved, just as they are.[2]

The yoke I was unable to bear was gone. No more chasing. Just as I am.

Accepted.

Permanence versus Performance

Being secure in the inner man means *permanently* resolving the acceptance issue.

Emphasis on the irreversible aspect of being fully accepted by God is essential. If God's acceptance is not eternal and absolutely guaranteed, then *we can lose it* the moment we do or don't do something. This is the crux of all our insecurities and fears: being uncertain about whether we are okay as men and human beings. Only an unequivocal declaration by someone who matters to us personally will put our souls at rest. That declaration, if believed, means no longer needing to make a name for ourselves, grab for false senses of power, or search for someone important to like us better than the next guy. We can stop comparing ourselves so much to others, being two-faced, and envying someone else's life. Forever acceptance puts an end to *all* of that.

Each of us needs the kind of moment Jesus experienced with his Father:

> As soon as Jesus was baptized, he went up out of the
> water. At that moment heaven was opened, and he saw
> the Spirit of God descending like a dove and alighting
> on him. And a voice from heaven said, "This is my Son,
> whom I love; with him I am well pleased."[3]

In this moment between God the Father and God the Son, we're given a model of what *every* man requires to live confidently versus insecurely: God's unconditional acceptance apart from performance. This event in Jesus' life is recorded early in Matthew's Gospel *before* . . .

- one message was preached
- one leper was cleansed
- one person was healed
- one mouth was fed
- one storm was calmed
- one dead person was raised
- one woman was defended
- one child was blessed
- one foot was washed
- one nail was absorbed
- one drop of blood was spilled

God's declaration of acceptance wasn't conditional or based on what his Son did; it was because of *whose Son he was*: "This is my Son." It was possessive, personal, and not performance based. Jesus went on to do many amazing things, but his energy and motivation for doing them weren't because he felt compelled or obligated. He did those things *because* he possessed the eternal and permanent validation of his Father. This moment of unconditional acceptance wasn't necessary for the Godhead; Father, Son, and Spirit modeled it because *this experience is meant for us*, whether it's public like Jesus' experience or private like mine. Whether our moments are public or private, we must simply note God's acceptance and seek to apply it to our own journeys.

What God models for us is meant for us.

Permanent acceptance without performance is the failsafe of the soul that comes with receiving God's love through the person and work of Christ, in the belief that his work on our behalf was *perfect.* When we accept this perfect act of love, we can stop performing for acceptance—permanently.

Jesus sensed it was time to begin his public ministry and presented himself to John for a baptism of repentance. Jesus' inner man was being drawn because God was laying on him an outer responsibility. He took the step God made available to him to act on, and God provided a public *and* personal moment for him.

In my own moment with God, I sensed something happening to me as well. Specifically, that culturally approved ways of securing worth, social status, and acceptance were leaving me less fulfilled, more empty, and at a loss to explain my dual existence (public and private) and lack of character in relationships. There was a growing body of internal and external evidence that I was stuck! So in response to what I was sensing, I took a step toward God the only way I knew how: by talking to him directly in prayer.

When you sense God's Spirit calling you into a moment, acting on it can be as simple as coming back to church, calling a trusted man of faith you respect, and being transparent about the struggle within. Whatever steps you take to address what's going on inside, you are setting up a faith moment God can use to reset you emotionally and spiritually through his love. Preceding your moment, you will sense through circumstances or the direct conviction of the Spirit of God that you are being called forward into an encounter with God's love.

When you take that bold, faith-filled step, the concerns you carry inside over your significance and worth are put to rest. The Bible declares that a "conquering" effect takes place: You no longer have to prove yourself to *anyone.*[4] We see this clearly in Jesus. In fact, people noticed how secure he was in the Father's acceptance and said to him, "You aren't swayed by others, because you pay no attention to who they are; but you teach the way of God in accordance with the truth."[5]

I remember after my own encounter with God's love that thoughts about how others perceived me were replaced with how God saw me. Practically, it appeared to others as a shift in my energies. I began putting less effort into earning social or professional capital and paying more attention to simple spiritual disciplines and serving God and others. It was also noticeable that I didn't need to check in and seek approval for my behavior or the activities I was engaged in. Call it being comfortable in your own skin, walking tall, feeling confident, or having inner security.

In the end, the way we know we haven't internalized and experienced God's unconditional acceptance is that we continue to care more about what other people think of us instead of being settled inside because God has accepted us.

Being "settled" simply means that the only person whose opinion *ultimately* matters to us becomes the one who drives our thinking and behavior. Why? Because the ultimate verdict on the ultimate issue has been rendered. God's man, like the Son of Man, is advancing God's purposes in his character and conduct without giving a single thought to fear of people. Fighting for the approval of others is over, and *living out of* God's acceptance and approval is moving forward.

Here is how believers are supposed to perceive themselves: When my son Ryan married my daughter-in-law, my relationship with her permanently changed. She became secure in her relationship with me and began to live in my permanent acceptance. I'm connected to her through my son. She loves Ryan, is committed to Ryan, and is one with Ryan. I love my son, and I love my daughter-in-law because of her connection to Ryan. His status with me is now her status with me: *fully accepted*. In a spiritual sense, she is "in" my son; she has accepted this acceptance and lives in it as a first-family member. She has all the status, rights, access, and privileges of a member of our family without the fear of ever losing them. On the day she and Ryan married, she got a new name. Her identity permanently became "Luck" on her driver's license and in my heart. I can't stop loving her until I stop loving my son—which will never happen!

God's acceptance of you won't stop until he stops loving his own Son.

I won't blame you if you read that sentence again—it's *everything* when it comes to the journey toward inner security and emotional health that God has all of us on. Practically, this means you're okay because God says you're okay, even when you're falling apart or feel unworthy. You are not "successful" as a man because you have your act together in front of other men; because of Jesus, you are accepted in spite of your failures or successes. Like me, you may have had a strong mental soaking in religion, which told you that God loves you because of what you do. That thinking needs to be consistently confronted, regularly replaced, and internally reinforced through repeated encounters with God's words about you. That's why this book is as much about spiritual battle as it is about spiritual growth. The mental minefield of self-perception must be retaken by marinating our hearts and minds in words that express the personal thoughts of God directly toward us. Of all the thoughts God thinks about us, the one he is hoping we'll work hard to internalize is this: *All performance has been replaced with permanent acceptance in Christ.*

Why is this priority one?

The wrong basis of acceptance by God produces the wrong experience in God. God's man will be forced to come back to this truth again and again on the journey toward inner security in Christ. Our fight for acceptance is over in God's mind, but the war within us must be resolved, and that involves a battle.

Spiritual Viruses

Fear is the Ebola of spiritual viruses that harms our life in God.

To see the spiritual connection, you have to understand why virologists have labeled Ebola the world's most deadly virus. Its high lethality is connected to the strategy of taking down our built-in defenses once it's inside the body. Specifically, the Ebola virus targets and attacks *one critical aspect* of our body's biochemistry. Remember that.

> *Once inside the bloodstream, the virus targets a compound called interferon. Interferon, named for its role in "interfering" with the virus' survival process, alerts the rest of the immune system to the presence of a foreign invader. Normally, interferon would deliver its warning message straight to the cell's command center via a special "emergency access lane."*
>
> *Ebola is too smart for that old trick.*
>
> *The virus hijacks the delivery process—preventing the immune system from organizing a coordinated attack—by attaching a bulky protein to the messenger. In its misshapen form, the messenger can't enter the cell. The immune system remains unaware of the problem, and the virus gets free range to attack and destroy the rest of the body. . . . [By the time] the immune system begins responding to the crisis in turbo mode . . . it's far too late. Rather than destroying the virus, our [immune] defenses simply rip our own bodies to shreds—from the inside out.*[6]

The messenger can't enter the cell. The virus is free to attack.

Fear is the Ebola of spiritual viruses because it attacks and hijacks the failsafe of God's unconditional acceptance in our lives, attaching lies to our faith in Christ. These lies block us from trusting in what God has already done, and they cause us to start trusting again in what we do or don't do. We move from permanent acceptance back to conditional performance. Fear is a tool of evil that separates our souls from resting in God's unconditional acceptance and cuts us off from the power his acceptance brings to our lives spiritually and emotionally. Believing the lies that fear attaches to our faith leads to a total breakdown of our emotional security, and those lies begin to eat our faith alive from the inside out. Similar to Ebola, fears within that are untouched by God's unconditional acceptance can be persistent, surviving for years, building up, and completely overtaking our vision of God, leading to destructive cycles of thinking and living. The inner spiritual and emotional security structures that God has given us have been compromised. Instead of living in the freedom of our full acceptance in Christ, we become free men who choose slavery.

If we don't resolve the acceptance issue once and for all . . .

We Live Fearfully

> Fear of man will prove to be a snare,
> but whoever trusts in the LORD is kept safe.
> Many seek an audience with a ruler,
> but it is from the LORD that one gets justice.[7]

Did you see the compare-contrast in these verses? Instead of living in the safety and security of God's acceptance, we allow people's opinions and acceptance of us to become the controlling influences in our lives. Fear sucks us into a vortex of synthetic worth connected to our social status or position in front of others, and we start channeling our energy toward their approval. The conditional acceptance of humans replaces God's unconditional acceptance and our real worth. We are no longer safe.

The permanence of God's acceptance loses to performing for people.

We Choose Foolishly

Many even among the leaders believed in [Jesus]. But because of the Pharisees they would not openly acknowledge their faith for fear they would be put out of the synagogue; for they loved human praise more than praise from God.[8]

Fear and foolish choices go hand in hand. To be seen, acknowledged, and accepted, we do things we normally wouldn't do. We say no to our faith and say yes to the acceptance of our friends, colleagues, or communities. We keep quiet instead of speaking up. We risk less for Jesus out in the open and retreat more. We go along with the group and engage in behaviors that we know fail to show love for God or people. Then we rationalize or spiritualize our wrong behavior, hiding behind God's grace or exercising our "liberty" in Christ.

Justification replaces Jesus.

We Act Immaturely and Behave Competitively

A dispute also arose among [the disciples] as to which of them was considered to be greatest. Jesus said to them, "The kings of the Gentiles lord it over them; and those who exercise authority over them call themselves Benefactors. But you are not to be like that Instead, the greatest among you should be like the youngest, and the one who rules like the one who serves.[9]

Fear of what others think and scarcity of attention cause men to compete for the limited commodity of visibility. Instead of resting secure in God's acceptance, we fear losing visibility. This fuels self-absorption, and we stop seeing people—their worth and their needs. It is head-scratching that men who had been walking with Jesus for three years (the disciples) fell into this trap of wanting personal visibility—when Jesus was standing right next to them! The created wanted to raise themselves above their Creator. The sheep dreamed of rising above the Shepherd. The clay entertained taking over from the Potter. Fear seized their hearts, and competition replaced connection among a group of Christ-following men!

Immaturity replaced maturity.

We Self-Destruct Relationally

> You, my brothers and sisters, were called to be free. But
> do not use your freedom to indulge the flesh; rather, serve
> one another humbly in love. For the entire law is fulfilled
> in keeping this one command: "Love your neighbor as
> yourself." If you bite and devour each other, watch out or
> you will be destroyed by each other.[10]

Our relationship stories reflect our personal inner stories at any given moment. Human history testifies that when fear is the foundation of any relationship, love is eroded and evil wins. Fear makes us compete for power, control, and our "rights." In the Garden of Eden, Satan's big plan to divide human beings from God and one another was simple: introduce fear into the relationship. Adam and

Eve were resting secure in God's love and acceptance until they were filled with the anxiety-producing thought that, somehow, *it wasn't enough.*

Some things never change. Satan knows that if he can make us feel anxious or cheated out of something, we'll make the same mistake Adam and Eve did. We'll stop believing what God says is true and start believing a lie.

Satan knows through experience that anxious people are bad at relationships. He knows we will protect ourselves and use the people we're supposed to be loving and serving to meet our perceived unmet needs. Other human beings become tools to make us feel less anxious, instead of people to build up, support, love, serve, and encourage. And when those same people feel used, whatever love they felt for us before will start turning to resentment. Over time, bitterness takes root, which will always manifest itself in divisive behaviors that destroy intimacy and trust.

Selfishness replaces serving one another.

The power of the gospel interrupts this domino effect. The exact opposite progression can be true if you believe, receive, accept, and internalize God's unconditional acceptance in Christ. Your supernatural failsafe will kick in and eliminate all of these security threats.

Instead, you will . . .

- live securely in his love and acceptance (versus insecurely);
- choose wisely out of that place of inner strength and security (versus foolishly);
- act maturely—being humbly confident in God's presence (versus immaturely);

- serve others in your relationships (versus behave selfishly); and
- advance intimacy and closeness (versus self-destruct relationally).

Eliminate the Threat

One of the most dangerous creatures on earth is an unvalidated man.

That bold and ominous statement is rooted in a simple fact: To know that one *matters* is a fundamental driving force for life. That spiritual and human reality presents us with a Pandora's box of cultural options that speak to and partially satisfy that need. Upward mobility is built around this need to matter, and it sounds something like this: Success leads to significance. There is a ladder of success, and if you climb it, eventually you will make it, which means you officially matter. Success is a crude but effective cultural weapon for winning validation. Culturally, you may achieve acceptance, but love and intimacy are ultimately lacking. The theater of battle is now complete, the pieces are now set, and the high-stakes game is afoot for the inner man. The results will be projected outwardly in your conduct, which will have consequences for others. On one side of the battle line is God's love and acceptance. On the other side are the rip-off versions of ultimate meaning and significance. Men live on both sides of the battle, and anyone connected to them experiences the healthy or unhealthy consequences of their respective paths to significance. Unvalidated men attempting to feel better about themselves routinely make unwanted headlines, and for the plurality of men whose social status isn't worthy of a headline, their choices are often seen in statistics.

Think about it for just a second. #METOO. Mass shootings.

Domestic violence. Divorce. Sexual slavery. Marital infidelity. Political corruption. Gang activity. Porn. The plague of fatherlessness. The orphan epidemic. Not to mention all of the emotional abuse that goes on behind closed doors that never sees the light of day or appears in a news headline. These outward expressions of male fear and self-loathing are just the tip of the iceberg. Hermit kingdoms, good-old-boy networks, cronyism in politics, and a host of systemic injustices also flow from an insidious and often unconscious force within—a lack of personal and permanent validation in Christ.

A lack of meaningful validation in men naturally leads to a vulnerability that evil can take advantage of to advance its agenda on earth. It explains, in part, how the evil one is able to wield so much power. He does it by lying to men about their worth, where it is ultimately found, and how it can be fostered. Behind the broken male culture is a feeling deep inside that something is missing, and we have to prove to ourselves that we are "the man." Ironically, the only thing we prove in all these instances of abuse, injustice, and acting out is that we are deeply afraid of never being valued and validated.

For these critical reasons, God wants all men to have a perfect and permanent failsafe against emotional insecurity and immaturity. He wants the security threat in *you* eliminated, especially if you claim an affiliation with Jesus Christ. It's time to leave the shallow waters of broken, divided, and diluted masculinity and faith and step into the fear-killing experience of *sonship* in God through Christ. To be adopted by God, brought into the family of God, all by the Son of God, changes everything.

God wants us to internalize and activate his approval and our sonship in three specific ways *right now*.

1. See God's Heart for You as Your Father

For a man, the strongest acceptance on planet earth is found in sharing a mutual love and connection with his father. Not only have I seen this prove true after ministering to millions of men over the past twenty years, but I've seen it in my own life as well. God wants every man to have a father who sees him, loves and accepts him unconditionally, and validates him as a man. That is the singular and most meaningful way God wants to relate to you. He wants you to see his heart for you as your heavenly Father. Jesus Christ has declared this, the Bible affirms it, and men from all over the world are experiencing the transforming power of that emotional bond with God as their failsafe against fear. Let God make it simple for you to decide.

> [God himself has] said,
> "How gladly would I treat you like [sons] . . .
> I thought you would call me 'Father'
>   and not turn away from following me."[11]

> Do not be like [unbelievers], for your Father knows what you need before you ask him. This, then, is how you should pray: "Our Father in heaven."[12]

According to Jesus, every man, regardless of age, needs a dad. He's offering his.

2. Openly Receive God's Acceptance and Respond to Him

God has taken the initiative to offer you his full and unconditional acceptance, but it hinges on one thing: fully and openly receiving that acceptance! It's called the *principle of reciprocity*. This occurs when two individuals see the value in something, reach a mutually beneficial agreement, and work together to make it happen.

When the Bible talks about God adopting us as sons into his family through Christ and allowing us to rise into first-family acceptance, a spiritual exchange occurs. This means that a two-way relational, emotional, and spiritual connection is established. More importantly, we recognize, appreciate, and above all, *openly receive his acceptance without reservation*. If you have a real reciprocal relationship with God, when he calls you his son, you will call him your Father in heaven, just as Jesus did. You will have the family resemblance. You will join the family of true sons. The Bible says that fear cannot compete with this connection, and this powerful Father-son bond ultimately defeats it.

> The Spirit you received does not make you slaves, so
> that you live in fear again; rather, the Spirit you received
> brought about your adoption to sonship. And by him we
> cry, "Abba, Father." The Spirit himself testifies with our
> spirit that we are God's children.[13]

3. Publicly Define Your Manhood by His Acceptance Alone

God's acceptance is the only acceptance a man should ever consider when determining what to believe and how to behave as a man. We check in with our Father, we look to our Father's face for approval, and we move forward only with his blessing.

His acceptance and love root all our decisions in him. His acceptance frees us to give love instead of being takers. His acceptance alone delivers disciplined consistency in all our choices, in all dimensions of our lives. Walking among men with an eye toward the Father's approval is the Jesus way, the family way. This way of living defeats fear. No obstacle in front of us is bigger than our Father, who is behind us as a man.

[Jesus said,] "The one who sent me is with me; he has not left me alone, for I always do what pleases him."[14]

In all . . . things we are more than conquerors through him who loved us.[15]

There is no fear in love. But perfect love drives out fear, because fear has to do with punishment. The one who fears is not made perfect in love.[16]

The Spirit God gave us does not make us timid, but gives us power, love and self-discipline.[17]

Every man needs a moment that facilitates the reality of God's ultimate acceptance. Like the moment when God modeled his acceptance at his Son's baptism, men down through the ages have needed to hear and internalize God speaking these words to them: "This is my [son], whom I love; with him I am well pleased."[18]

Unfortunately, most men have not received that needed blessing from another man in their lives, and even more have not realized that this missing piece in their souls drives much of their identity and energy. But God is waiting for all of us to enter into a moment of acceptance and blessing with him. He wants that experience of receiving his blessing to flow into us in powerful, emotional, and life-altering ways. It's a moment of recognition as well as release. We recognize that God the Father made us to be loved by him. We recognize false forms of validation and replace them with ultimate validation in him. We recognize that through God's caring presence in our lives, a monumental battle for our inner man has been won permanently. The act of recognition leads to a necessary release of lesser forms of acceptance and validation that promised meaning and significance but ultimately could not deliver them.

Sonship in God ends the search for significance.

It also marks the beginning of a new journey.

If your desire is sonship and God's full acceptance, his desire is to be your Father in every way and eliminate the threat fear poses in your life. Every person ever created not only seeks but needs that comfort and assurance of their worth to prevent them from living out of the lack of it emotionally. If it's your desire to resolve the acceptance issue permanently and activate the failsafe of God's acceptance, it's time to accept and affirm your sonship with God by applying the three things he requires.

Use this prayer to express, or perhaps affirm, your desire for active sonship with him.

Father in heaven,

I see your heart for me, and I'm grateful. Thank you for making a way through Christ to have your love and your Spirit in my life. I receive your love for me and accept my name as your son. I receive the Spirit of adoption into your family, and I receive the validation that comes with it. I receive your declaration of my identity in you and my inheritance in you eternally. Fill me with the Spirit of sonship for the world to see. I reject the fear of man and, from this moment forward, will let your love for me define me until I am with you in our home in heaven.

In Jesus' name, I accept, I affirm, and I declare my sonship in you. Amen.

2

YOU WOULD DO THAT FOR ME?

I Am Fully Loved

SHOCKING. Overwhelming. Convincing.

As I watch this short video on my computer, my mouth is hanging open and my breath is getting cut off. The visual is *that* unnerving and powerful. I'm watching an abnormally massive wall of water form out of the sea, and then—for scale—I see a tiny Jet Ski towing an even tinier speck of a man across the top of the developing face of a behemoth wave. I'm in the safety of my own kitchen, sipping coffee, with nothing to fear. But at this moment, my eyes are bulging, my mind is racing, and my heart is pounding. I'm nervously waiting for what is about to happen next, because I've seen video of other big-wave riders who either don't surface or float limply in the water and need CPR administered to them on the shore after being thrown into these hydraulic hurricanes known in the surfing world as "big rollers."

The tiny speck of a man now letting go of the towrope at the top of this moving skyscraper is Brazilian Rodrigo Koxa. He doesn't know it now, but the wave he has decided to tame off the coast of Portugal is an eighty-foot wall of water. If he survives, it will be the largest ocean wave ever surfed.[1] My eyes are straining to see where Koxa is, and then I spot a familiar white streak of board fins breaking the water as he begins to accelerate down the face of the wave. At this moment, there appears to be a lot of space between him and the dangerous lip of the wave that will soon catch up to him. He is streaking across this giant water canvas when, as expected, the wave starts to turn over, and gravity pulls the massive lip onto the shallower waters below. Here it comes. A mountain of churning white water begins to cascade and explode behind Koxa, closing fast. My heart rate picks up again as I wonder if he can possibly outsurf the danger about to swallow him.

Although he is traveling an estimated fifty miles per hour, it's not fast enough, and he disappears into the splintering blast zone occurring at the lower base of this wave. *It's over* is my next thought. Then, miraculously, out of the white jaws I thought had consumed him, a black speck emerges, and this Brazilian daredevil is gliding smoothly out of harm's way. Elapsed time? Fourteen seconds from the moment he let go of the towrope to the moment he surfed out of the white water, both feet still inserted in the heavy-duty loops built into his specially designed board. The official measurement confirmed that Koxa broke the world record on November 8, 2017, for the largest wave ever surfed in the history of humankind. Look it up, and you'll see what I mean.

No fellow surfer can ever question Rodrigo Koxa's passion or commitment to the sport of surfing. Ever. Ever. Ever! Why not? One simple reason: *The most committed person is the one who takes the biggest risks and makes the biggest sacrifices.* Risk and sacrifice are the universal indicators of ultimate commitment. We don't need data or deep analysis to back it up. We know it immediately when we see it. It's obvious. The most committed people do radical things to confirm their passion for the object of their affection.

Could be surfing. Or, just for fun, it could be sushi! Sound goofy? Hold your rainbow roll. In January of 2019, a Japanese "sushi boss" broke his own previous record of $1.4 million for a single tuna by paying $3.1 million for a 612-pound bluefin tuna at the opening of Tokyo's new fish market.[2] All that money so a man named Kiyoshi Kimura could keep his coveted "Tuna King" title. I cannot fathom that. But to our point here, when it comes to commitment, people take extraordinary risks and will pay the ultimate price for their greatest loves. Rodrigo Koxa loves surfing so deeply that he would put everything on the line for that one wave. Kiyoshi Kimura loves the sushi business and his status within it so fully that he would plunk down the equivalent of a home along the coast in Malibu for a dead fish. What we may think is radical and over the top is natural for the überpassionate. It may be shocking. It may appear excessive or overwhelming. But you can't deny it. This kind of committed passion is convincing and worth emulating as we explore God's love for us.

Personal, authentic passion for anything or anyone inspires risk and sacrifice.

"You Would Do That for Me?"

I was young. I was poor. But I was falling passionately in love.

On this day I found myself sitting across the table from the woman who, just four years later, would become Christine Luck. At this early stage of my relationship with Chrissy, my feelings were like the SpaceX solid-rocket system after initial liftoff. I was in the process of jettisoning my initial-stage feelings and transitioning to the more powerful second-stage solid-rocket booster of right-brain feelings that would take me into outer space. I'm not sure if my eyes told the full story, but I was trying to play it cool and not show just how "in the juice" I was for her. As we talked, she told me about a jacket she fell in love with when she saw it in a store next to campus. She wanted it, but it was too expensive.

"Really," I said. "Tell me more!" What she couldn't see was me scribbling notes on a napkin I had slyly snuck under the table. I empathized with her plight. Then I asked her what kind of jacket it was. Did they have her size? Did the store ever have sales? Mission accomplished. Secret notes taken, I excused myself, saying I had a political science class I had to attend (a lie). We parted, she to attend her afternoon classes, and me to the bank to withdraw the cost of a white denim jacket.

When she walked into her bedroom after class and plopped on her bed, her eyes locked onto the fancy white bag with a perfect brown bow nestled beside her pillows. Attached to the bag was a note. Inside was the object of her affection. When we met up later, her words confirmed she got the message I was attempting to send.

She said, "You would do that for me?"

Are you sensing what I'm stepping into? Commitment rising. Love growing. New risks being taken. Sacrifices communicating my heart. Putting myself on the line. I shocked her. I overwhelmed her. I convinced her there was more to the gesture than a size 4 white denim jacket. The look in her eye and what happened next told me she understood.

Isn't that the goal of any relationship or pursuit we care deeply about? We want people to know we'll "make the drop" to catch what we feel is the biggest wave in the world, the biggest bluefin tuna ever caught, or the most phenomenal woman any man could ever hope for.

When you're pursuing a relationship, you want to secure space in a woman's heart. You want your message received in her spirit.

You want what is inside you to reside securely and confidently inside her, and it is only through risk and sacrifice that the message of your full commitment is conveyed.

The question Chrissy asked is not just a fitting bow to tie off a "nice" story. These words are for us when we think of Jesus Christ and consider the fullness, completeness, and genuineness of his sacrificial love toward us. When we ponder what he did for us, we have only one response: "You would do that for me?"

> Before the Passover celebration, Jesus knew that his hour had come to leave this world and return to his Father. He had loved his disciples during his ministry on earth, and now he loved them to the very end. It was time for supper, and the devil had already prompted Judas, son of Simon Iscariot, to betray Jesus. Jesus knew that the Father had given him authority over everything and that he had come from God and would return to God. So he got up from the table, took off his robe, wrapped a towel around his waist, and poured water into a basin. Then he began to wash the disciples' feet, drying them with the towel he had around him.[3]

You would do that for me?

> [Jesus said,] "I am the good shepherd. The good shepherd lays down his life for the sheep."[4]

You would do that for me?

> Going a little farther, he fell with his face to the ground and prayed, "My Father, if it is possible, may this cup be taken from me. Yet not as I will, but as you will."[5]

You would do that for me?

> Christ's love compels us, because we are convinced
> that one died for all, and therefore all died. And he
> died for all, that those who live should no longer live
> for themselves but for him who died for them and was
> raised again.[6]

There it is. Let it sit there. Take a breath. Be nervous. Be excited. But above all, be at peace. That's what Jesus wants for you. You are fully, pervasively, and specifically loved for being you. Don't look around in this moment. Just look into his face, react with your whole person, and say to Jesus, "You would do that for me?"

Say it as many times as you need to say it until it happens. Until what happens? Until the assurance of his affection for you rests securely and confidently inside you.

His answer? "*Yes, I would do that for you. You are so worth it.*" He *so loves* you. Let it in. You are his passion, the one he went to the greatest lengths to secure. That's the truth about you. It should be as shocking and overwhelming to you as it is convincing. And you should respond with energy, emotions, tears, awe, worship, and wonder.

Jesus went to radical lengths to accomplish a radical thing. He chose you. Not because you merited anything in yourself. He simply looked at you and said, "*I love him.*" And to quiet any fears you might have that he could change his mind, he did something very weighty, very risky, and very final that you can always fall back on when any circumstance or situation allows doubt about his love to creep into your thinking.

He died for you.

Facta, non Verba

Facta, non verba is Latin for "actions, not words." I am one of those guys who believe that strong actions send the clearest messages. As a basketball player, I used to get elbows to the face from teammates and opponents alike. Those hits were *not* accidental. The message was loud and clear: "You are playing me too close, and you can do that, but this is what is going to happen if you do." And the dance went on. In high school on Valentine's Day, veiled love notes were put in the school paper that said things like "To my dreamy surfer boy in Mr. Pugh's government class. You are my personal Valentine. Love, Your Blue-bindered Admirer." And then at morning recess and lunch, pockets of eager boys and girls formed to decode, decipher, and gather intelligence to identify the mysterious messenger.

I grew up watching movies about the mafia where sending a message to a rival crime family was an art form—and usually bloody. That was the whole idea. Brutal action, not words. No talking. No texting. No DMing. No Zoom calls. Just a simple "Say hello to my little friend" and a staccato spray of bullets everywhere.

Less morbid and way more fun to watch are romantic comedies (rom-coms) with a predictable dilemma: "Does she know that he likes her?" Then you spend the next ninety minutes watching two people miss each other's signals, commiserate with their best friends, try again, and fail in a funny way two or three more times. Finally, the main characters get painted into a corner. Some bad guys are about to kill them, or one of the main characters is at the altar about to say "I do" to the wrong person, and at that precarious moment, the truth finally comes out, to everyone's relief.

Key word? *Relief.*

It's a relief to know the truest truth once and for all. That way you can start to make the important relationship decisions you need to make about whether to stay or go, commit or quit, invest or cut your losses. "Sort of" knowing is not knowing. It's frustrating. We want the truest truth in our relationships because it reflects reality versus a mystery that remains emotionally elusive. It's also why this journey into locking down your inner man and getting secure in God's love is so important. Not knowing it deeply, not internalizing it emotionally, not seeing it personally, not applying it psychologically and spiritually spells frustration and destruction in the midst of the unplanned losses and unwelcome adversities this world dishes up. All of the tribulations Jesus said would come have the capacity to throw us off in our relationship with God and people if we become unsure and insecure with respect to his love toward us. Worse, we become vulnerable to seeking cheap forms of relief rather than standing in the truest truth that circumstances may impact our lives, but they don't impact how much God loves us. Really? That black-and-white? Yes. That is the gospel Jesus brought to earth and lived out in front of our eyes.

If God's love was present, moving, redeeming, saving, and delivering us as his Son was being tortured and crucified, then his love is easily present with us in every circumstance. More importantly, his love is similarly accomplishing God's purposes whether or not we see it, feel it, or recognize it. This offers both relief and clarity to any follower of Jesus when it comes to God's love and our circumstances. It was God's love that energized the decision for Jesus to leave heaven and come to earth. It was God's love that allowed Jesus to take on all injustices, all sin, and all evil and use it all for good. No one felt it was good in the moment or loved seeing Jesus' back turned to shredded meat. No disciple had relief or clarity when the people shouted for Pilate to release Barabbas instead of Jesus. No onlooker saw God's unfailing love happening when Jesus was spilling his blood on the Via Dolorosa. And certainly, no one who stood on the lonely hill outside Jerusalem saw that love at work while watching the most compassionate man who ever walked this earth suffer through a Roman crucifixion. No one witnessing these events was aware that God was *so loving us* in the midst of them.

Hardships in this life will attack and diminish the solid assurance of God's act of love for us. Time will attack that assurance. Forgetting what he did will attack that assurance. Our perception that God is distant will attack it. Overwhelming pain will mute it. But God's act of love is always there, always an anchor for us to cling to in the middle of our darkness. It's a reminder that he knows what suffering feels like. It's a true connection with our pain, because he himself has suffered pain on our behalf. This is why we turn to this act of love. This is why we let it sink in so deeply. This is why we let his act of love move us from despair to hope. Hurt speaks to hurt unlike easy platitudes and lofty religious-speak. The strength of God's sacrificial love doesn't eliminate the pains of earth; rather, it promises to redeem those same pains in a meaningful way. This is God's promise to you right now.

So, what do you think? With God on our side like this, how can we lose? If God didn't hesitate to put everything on the line for us, embracing our condition and exposing himself to the worst by sending his own Son, is there anything else he wouldn't gladly and freely do for us? And who would dare tangle with God by messing with one of God's chosen? Who would dare even to point a finger? The One who died for us—who was raised to life for us!—is in the presence of God at this very moment sticking up for us. Do you think anyone is going to be able to drive a wedge between us and Christ's love for us? There is no way! Not trouble, not hard times, not hatred, not hunger, not homelessness, not bullying threats, not backstabbing, not even the worst sins listed in Scripture. . . .

None of this fazes us because Jesus loves us. I'm absolutely convinced that nothing—nothing living or dead, angelic or demonic, today or tomorrow, high or low, thinkable or unthinkable—absolutely nothing can get between us and God's love because of the way that Jesus our Master has embraced us.[7]

That is the "gospel of no matter what." No matter what befalls you, attacks you, discourages you, diminishes you, wounds you, or creates losses for you, nothing can diminish the quality or quantity of God's love in your life. His love is present, it's at work, and it is accomplishing his purposes his way. The love God has shown for you in Christ has earned your implicit trust and settled confidence. You are secure inside because of his never-changing love for you. Think about that for a moment.

Nothing can dilute God's love for you. He doesn't love you more when you get it right or love you less when you fall short. That is the message of this prayer:

I pray that you, being rooted and established in love, may have power, together with all the Lord's holy people, to grasp how wide and long and high and deep is the love of Christ, and to know this love that surpasses knowledge— that you may be filled to the measure of all the fullness of God.[8]

When we grasp Christ's love by seeing how he personally risked and sacrificed to communicate our worth, nothing can diminish the impact or intention of that love. We will dive even deeper into this later, but for now just know that Jesus' love doesn't track up or down with your performance.

Nothing can separate you from God's affection. If you believe that nothing separated Jesus from God's love when he walked this earth—not adversity, not injustice, not even death on the cross— then you know for certain that whatever life may throw at you, the same thing is true for you. You take in the courage that this truest truth provides. In every challenge you face in your life right now and in the future, Jesus fully assures you that his loving presence will be with you.

> I have told you these things, so that in me you may have peace. In this world you will have trouble. But take heart! I have overcome the world.[9]

Jesus shot straight with his followers on the downside of living on an unredeemed planet, but he also highlighted the upside of knowing him in the midst of the downside. Specifically, Jesus said we'll have trouble in this life on earth. Things that happen to you will feel unjust at times. You'll spend energy trying to avoid pain, suffering, and loss, and just when you think everything is lining up—*kaboom!* A pandemic. Injustice and evil in the streets. Division and political chaos.

You take a wonderful exit after a long career and get a bummer health diagnosis.

You tell your friend today, "The marriage has never been better." Then—*wham!*—you come home to empty drawers in your master bedroom, a note from your spouse, and a wedding ring on the dresser.

You find out that a close friend or family member recently committed suicide.

Jesus himself tells us to *expect* moments like these in life. He doesn't desire them, but he knows they will come into our lives until he sets earth and the hearts of people straight again. Jesus says to his followers that loss and pain are inevitable in this world, but despair and anxiety are optional. We have the "Take heart!" promise going for us, which changes the game in this world we are trying to navigate. Jesus is speaking directly to the habit of men allowing negative circumstances to define our outlook on life, on ourselves, and on our future. Then, in one strong statement, he declares that we are not defined by our negative experiences. Instead we're defined by the truest truth: His very person transcends our circumstances and builds a bridge from panic to courage in him.

As God's "so loved" ones, we expect that our plans might get knocked over or eliminated, but never God's love. That is always consistent. Always present. Always working around the bitter to bring the sweet.

Nothing can distract God's focused attention and affection from you. Think of something you see every day. Grass. Cement. Pigeons. People. Cars. Traffic. In Southern California, we see fifteen different types of sparrows in addition to forty million people and the traffic that creates. Sparrows are common birds that don't particularly stand out like some other notable birds, such as the turkey vulture or red hawk. Why the Audubon Society lesson? In our global ecosystem consisting of more than seven billion people, we can easily feel lost and uncared for at times. You might be taking care of others, but you hear this voice say, "Who's taking care of you?" Then you hear that same voice offer a suggestion or solution to tough times that would violate your love for God or others. You may think that God must be distracted when it comes to you, your personal situation, and how alone you feel in it. Sound familiar?

This is when you must remind yourself of the truest truth that transcends the mundane truth you see with your eyes:

> Are not two sparrows sold for a penny? Yet not one of
> them will fall to the ground outside your Father's care.
> And even the very hairs of your head are all numbered.[10]

> My soul yearns, even faints,
>> for the courts of the LORD. . . .
>> LORD Almighty, my King and my God.
> Blessed are those who dwell in your house;
>> they are ever praising you.[11]

You may not feel that anyone notices you, but that doesn't mean someone doesn't care deeply about you and for you. One day we won't have this battle, but between now and then, God is reasserting his care for you and his full awareness of what is happening in your life. Receive his care now in faith. You have a home. You have a Father who sees you and loves you. You have full access to his house right now. Start talking to him and receiving his love, which is focused on you this very second!

No "thing" can conquer you internally, because of God's affection for you. The number-one benefit of God's love in your life is its ability to conquer fear and anxiety, sadness and anger, loneliness and isolation. As a mental-health worker and pastor, I have spoken with thousands of people who struggle with all of these problems. Some of these people have genetic issues and chemical imbalances. Others have dysfunctional family-system and environmental dynamics that drive their issues. Some have none of those issues but simply make choices that negatively affect their physical and mental health. Usually, some combination of factors work together to cause problems. In spite of all these obstacles, it's stunning to me how the majority of people can be helped in a powerful way by identifying how they received love and comfort in their emotionally formative years.

Follow me.

Love and comfort communicate worth. Worth that is felt and internalized produces peace and security instead of anxiety and doubts about our worth. That isn't to say that people who are loved and comforted well in childhood don't experience stress and anxiety later on. But I can safely observe that those who experienced a secure attachment with a parent or other adult growing up have a significantly better chance of handling the ups and downs of life more successfully than those who don't. For those with a secure childhood attachment, love and comfort in the midst of fears and unknowns were generously expressed, which mitigated fear's damaging, long-term hold on them. Fear in the moment was allayed.

Unexpected losses, unplanned difficulties, and unwelcome pain also enter our lives as God's beloved children. How can we experience the same kind of love and comfort a hurting child needs in the moment? Think about a child's response, and you'll discover a simple road map to experiencing God's love and comfort.

- Children cry out in a moment of pain or panic. They react emotionally to the pain and don't hide the fact that they've been injured or feel fear. It's an unscripted, unrehearsed reaction that no loving parent questions or analyzes. A child may scream in agony, shout "Mommy!" or "Daddy!", or run as fast as she can to hide behind a parent. The warrior David described this exact scenario, saying of God, "He turned to me and heard my cry!"[12] As God's child, David cried out when he needed God's help, comfort, or love—or all three at once. Crying out to God was a repeated theme in David's life, and it's a model for us.

- Children allow examination and assessment in a moment of pain or panic. A loving parent may ask questions like "What happened?" or "Where does it hurt?" or "Who did this to you?" These kinds of questions are natural and necessary. The difference in our relationship with God is that he has already seen what transpired, but for us to receive his love and comfort requires the reciprocal exchange of information. Not for God, but for us. Knowing he has seen the events and interactions of our lives in full detail already, when we reveal or confess the true nature of our fears or real sources of our pain to him, we can begin to heal and overcome the problem *with him*. He sees it. We see it. We see it together. He can now step toward us with our full awareness to apply comfort and love.

- Children open themselves to the presence, promise, and power of a parent or guardian whose mission is to love and comfort them. That person assures them, "It's going to be okay." Have you ever told a child this? Did you ever hear these words from someone you trust? In pain or panic, the emotional weight and import of that simple statement is like a spiritual IV line that rushes peace into our hearts in the midst of our pain. Sometimes parents don't even have to say anything. Just an awareness of their presence is enough for a child, because their presence is their promise and power all in one. At other times, assurance through higher insight is calming. Still other moments call for a necessary action that doesn't allay fear or lessen pain but ensures that the pain has a good purpose. Telling my then-four-year-old son in the ER, "Your dad's here, and it's going to be okay" did not stop the medical team from injecting charcoal through a nasogastric tube into his stomach to soak up the medicine

53

he guzzled. But he went from a bright-red face and shaking body to normal coloration and calm *in the midst of* a terrifying procedure for him.

God gave us his Son so that we could have access to permanent love and pervasive comfort. Full assurance of God's love means worth and relief, but it also means power. Relief means we can stop wondering whether we are enough or acting out of what we feel we lack. Power means we put that energy toward faith in God's presence and care, as well as taking faith-filled steps toward him in the midst of our challenges. Love and comfort are transactional. We turn to our Father first. We cry out to him. We seek him out. We hear him out. We take in his words with the confidence and faith of a child. We rest secure in the midst of the pain and the process. We take in courage through his love and comfort. We overcome.

Those close to us see God's love translating into a true and attractive boldness that shines the light of Christ into the big and small spaces of our lives. Listen to what a fully loved man who is secure in God's love said in the midst of his journey on earth: "In all [our troubles] we are more than conquerors through him who loved us."[13]

This is me. I have things in my life and background that I would rather not have. Mental illness. Suicide. Incarceration. A fast-approaching and unknown future. Spiritual attacks. Relational challenges. Crippling pressures at times that make for many sleepless nights. Some people think they want my life. They say, "You're so blessed with your family and what God allows you to see and do." They would be right, because I do have an enviable life if you look at it through a social media lens. But what they really see and want is the reward of persevering through much pain and suffering, believing in, internalizing, and being fully assured of God's love and comfort in the midst of hell. What they don't know is that alongside those blessings and rewards have come great losses and abiding challenges. This is where the rubber of God's love meets the road of my challenges. Because we share this pilgrim experience here on earth, I am going to say with confidence that this is your crossroads too.

Know this, my brother: God is keeping careful watch over you and your future. The day is coming when you'll have it all—life healed and whole.

I know how great this makes you feel, even though you have to put up with every kind of aggravation in the meantime. Pure gold put in the fire comes out of it proved pure; genuine faith put through this suffering comes out proved genuine. When Jesus wraps this all up, it's your faith, not your gold, that God will have on display as evidence of his victory.

You never saw him, yet you love him. You still don't see him, yet you trust him—with laughter and singing. Because you kept on believing, you'll get what you're looking forward to: total salvation.[14]

Here are a few imperfect words when there are no words for what Jesus did for us:

Jesus,

Your love for me is shocking. What you faced and endured for me—I have no words. I am overwhelmed because I know who I am and I know who you are, and I struggle to put those two together. Your love and justice came together for me perfectly at the cross. It was a tender and brutal kiss I am seeing once again. I am letting myself feel it once again. I am letting it hit me and heal me. I never have a reason to doubt your love for me because of what you did and how the Father used it to redeem and save me. I see with eyes of faith, that is how you are working right now in my life, and I declare your love and faithfulness over all of my life—even the challenges right now that make me vulnerable to other voices. I need your love and comfort in places you already see. I see those broken places too. I am seeing it with you. Wash my heart again of fear and worry through your presence inside me. Fill me with the Holy Spirit and produce new faith, new hope, new peace, and the new boldness of a conqueror. Your love is my peace, and that peace makes me bold for you. Thank you for your eternal commitment to me. I see it, I feel it, I am letting it sink all the way into me, and I am so grateful. Amen.

3

SOMEONE HAS TO DIE

I Am Fully Defined

SOMETHING IS MISSING.

We watch. We compare. We analyze the "playground." We look the part. We focus on saying the right things, wearing the right things, doing the right things. We compete hard. We train hard not to lose ground. We invest time. We are loyal. We pay our dues. We seek promotions. We get knocked down but get up faster than we fell. It hurt when we fell, but nobody will ever know. We aren't going to complain. Not us. We pursue. We chase. We possess. We build new things, and we build on what we have built. Then we find new things to chase. We set goals. We execute the plan. We add value. We work late. We go the second mile. We build relational capital. We make money. We win, and when we lose we say, "Failure is just success turned inside out." But the failure makes us question ourselves.

Where does it end?

But, hey, we have friends. We have church. We have neighbors. We have family. We have "followers." We tweet. We have political opinions. We have cable news. We have HD-streaming screens (plural). We are up on sports. We have our teams. We are general managers of "teams." We have hobbies. We have gear connected to our hobbies—oh, do we have gear. We know the Amazon driver personally. We know the barista. We know the waitress at the bar. We got a guy for everything. They're all in our contacts. Need one? We got a car guy. We got a mortgage guy. We got a contractor guy. We got a mechanic guy. We got a tickets guy. We are connected. We entertain. We vacation. We tailgate. We go out to eat. We appreciate nice things. We have our classic music mixes. We podcast. We socialize. We exercise. We relax well. We do craft beer. We do cigars. We groove. We do Boutique-y Whisky—or we used to do that kinda thing, but it became a problem. In that case, we do club soda. We are in control now. We know what matters. We even know right from wrong. How are we doing? Is that even a question? "Honestly?" we reply. "I'm tired, but it's a good tired." Then the alarm goes off so we can get "good tired" again.

All that output. All that energy. All that work. We tell ourselves it means something. But we aren't convinced deep down. Without some context, is anything meaningful?

We are restless.

We know we are restless because we're discontent. We know we are restless because our plates are full-full-full, but we go to sleep feeling empty, anxious about the emptiness, and alone in our struggles. We know we are restless because even though we're surrounded by family and friends, by good things, by our stuff, and by things to do next, we *feel* lonely. But no one knows. Keeping up appearances is draining emotionally. We know we are restless because we say things like "It is what it is," but we don't really believe that. We just don't want to talk about it. We are the most connected, the most communicative, the most technologically advanced generation ever, but at the same time, we are the most inwardly disconnected and fragmented we have ever been. It's confusing at a deep level to have so much going on and feel lost inside a private world *we chose to build*.

The world is making us better off but not better.

Our bodies, our mouths, our fingers, and our eyes are constantly moving and responding to our screens, our schedules, our responsibilities, and the demands of relationships. In the middle of all that stimuli and running around, we wonder, *Where is all this effort headed? What does it all mean? Does it count? Is this what being alive means? Does any of it have purpose?* Because if not, we are not really living. We're just dying and looking really busy in the process. We want to know that giving our time, energies, and resources truly counts for something beyond us.

If you've ever felt any of these feelings, you are not alone. We all need to know the why behind the what of our lives. The Bible shares the testimony of a guy who literally had everything his senses and interests craved, and he was still looking, just like you and me.

> I took a good look at everything I'd done, looked at
> all the sweat and hard work. But when I looked, I saw
> nothing but smoke. Smoke and spitting into the wind.
> There was nothing to any of it. Nothing.[1]

The not knowing exhausts us. But worse, it makes us insecure and afraid.

How come? Because, eventually, the smoke must clear.

All for All, Some for Some, None for None

To really live and feel fully alive, Jesus said that someone has to die.

> [Jesus] called the crowd to him along with his disciples and said: "Whoever wants to be my disciple must deny themselves and take up their cross and follow me. For whoever wants to save their life will lose it, but whoever loses their life for me and for the gospel will save it."[2]

What is life really all about? Not our activities. No—it's about loss of life.

No use softening the blow. Jesus was telegraphing what it means for all would-be followers to experience the full potential of this relationship. In today's environment, his marketing people would have scrubbed this direct style and approach. Not exactly the best way to cast a wide recruiting net for a global movement and an attractive future. Thankfully, the only consideration for Jesus was truth being spoken in love—even if it left a mark or followers left him. It was the right time for a cup of brutal, life-altering honesty—no cream or sugar to smooth it out or soften its strength.

It reminds me of a Haitian preacher who came to our church in Orange County, California. After beginning his message and making his first few points about how through Christ "all things are possible," he sensed a disconnect between himself and his audience (a group of people who spend more on gourmet coffee in one year than a Haitian earns from a full-time yearly salary). The body language in the crowd kindled a fire inside him, and you could see something happening behind his deep-brown eyes. A long pause filled the crowded room. Then the velvet of his Creole accent through a translator turned into the steel of his own very pointed, convicting, and strained English. No use softening the blow.

"I don't think you understand what Jesus has done for you," he said. It was off-putting, and the temperature of the room changed immediately. Eyebrows furrowed. Smiles disappeared. Into this awkwardness and silence, he continued with simple words in his third-best language. "Because if you *really* understood what Jesus has done for you, you would be jumping up and down and out of your seats. You would be moving and shaking and dancing and shouting and celebrating with me. I think you are too comfortable."

Here we go.

"Say this with me," he continued. "'All for all.'"

The crowd responded in unison, "All for all."

Then he said, "Now say, 'some for some.'"

"Some for some" was the unified response.

"Now say, 'none for none,'" he followed.

"None for none" came back as expected.

The final call was, "Now say it all together: 'All for all. Some for some. None for none.'"

"All for all. Some for some. None for none" flooded the room.

Target now acquired. Missiles now locked. Time to press the red button.

"When you give *none of yourself* to God," he began, "you receive nothing in return from God."

Okay. Got it.

Building on this thought, he then said, "When you give *some of yourself* to God, you get some of God in return. But when you give *all of yourself* to God, you get all of God in return. You choose your experience with God. All for all. Some for some. None for none.

"Which experience are you? All for all? Some for some? Or none for none?"

The figurative pink elephant in the room—or, if you prefer, the eight-hundred-pound spiritual gorilla in the room—was now sitting on our collective chest. This Haitian preacher was forcing us to reflect on the strength of our identification with Christ, what he did for us, and the implications of each. Implicit was the idea that we were "somewhat identified with Christ," and that reality was reflected in every dimension of our worship and our faith expression, as well as in our inner person. The Holy Spirit through this courageous Haitian pastor was doing his work or, rather, was working us over!

It goes without saying that no follower of Jesus, when contemplating a face-to-face encounter with him, wants to be a some-for-some member of the team. Every believer wants to be in the all-for-all category, living out an all-for-all commitment, possessing all-for-all stories that validate their fullest allegiance and identity in this life. Jesus' love calls for that. So with that future moment and motivation clearly in view, how is it that those God fully accepts and fully loves cannot *fully identify* ourselves with Christ? Why can't we let his love go all the way to the center of who we are and eliminate all fear of commitment? Think about it. Up to this point in our journey, we know that because of God's love, we don't need to chase earthly validation. We are fully accepted and free to live for an audience of one. We also know we don't ever have to doubt his commitment to us in the midst of any circumstance. The gospel says we are fully loved; Jesus has secured our confidence forever though his radical and passionate act.

But now, both the greatest challenge to and the greatest accelerator of our inner security through God's love present themselves: Will we allow Jesus' act of love to fully define us so that we live for God with reckless abandon and full faith? As Jesus did, will we actually surrender ourselves in a moment of absolute trust to God's total invasion of our identity with his love and turn our future over to him? Are we ready to go all the way with Jesus to the end of this journey without knowing all the implications? Are we courageous enough to enter the all-for-all experience with God's love?

If our response is yes, the act of Christ's love for us now becomes the basis of the actions we ourselves must take to secure and seal our hearts forever in his love.

> If we have died with Christ, we believe that we shall also live with Him, knowing that Christ, having been raised from the dead, is never to die again; death no longer is master over Him. For the death that He died, He died to sin once for all; but the life that He lives, He lives to God. Even so consider yourselves to be dead to sin, but alive to God in Christ Jesus.[3]

"*Even so?*" Did you catch that connective ligament that tethers you as a Christ follower to his radical act of commitment for you? It's a bridge from him to you that animates God's love in your life in the most real and powerful way. It is God telling you how his act of love—what happened on the cross and what ensued after Jesus gave up his life—can now happen *in you* and spread to every facet of your life, infusing it with his intended purpose and meaning. It narrows life down to the simple pursuits of seeing yourself the way God sees you and believing it enough to choose it. You don't have to be *that* person anymore, because God's act of love is defining you, your choices, and your purpose. The person formerly known as you has been replaced spiritually and is free to confidently embrace a new hunger for God's will and purposes. We cannot miss this, or we'll miss the power of the gospel in our lives.

God's act of love declares that you are dead to sin and alive to God.

Remember the Haitian pastor's words? "*I don't think you understand what Jesus has done for you.*" Christians who fail to internalize God's love and apply what he wants it to accomplish in their identity inevitably end up trying to blend their old lives with their new lives in Christ. Every believer knows what this means in some way. Every one of us has ways of thinking and acting that are hard to give up, get rid of, or surrender. It could be a habit, a way of thinking about certain issues, a long-burning resentment, anxiety connected to trauma in our past, or an emotional attachment to certain people that is unhealthy. What falls into that category in your life? Examining whatever divides your lifestyle from your faith is a good way to identify things that God says you're "dead" to now. It shouldn't be hard to figure out those things. In your head you rationalize them. You justify them. You excuse them. Or, worse, you blame someone else for them.

If you want to see how silly attempting to blend our old lives with our new lives looks to God, stream the 1980s comedy *Weekend at Bernie's.*[4] At the invitation of their boss, Bernie, a couple of insurance-company employees—Richard and Larry—stay at his ritzy beach house for the weekend. The guys had alerted Bernie to serious embezzlement in the company, but they have no idea that Bernie is behind it, or that he is planning to kill them, a scheme that backfires when Bernie himself becomes the victim of a hit man. Determined not to ruin their weekend, Richard and Larry go to hilarious lengths to make it look like Bernie is still alive. They devise ways to physically prop up the dead guy at parties, in the car, and on the beach, all in full view of other people who are curious about Bernie's condition. The problem with their plan is that the corpse doesn't cooperate! It slumps. It falls over. It hits things as it falls, calling attention to itself and its sidekicks. The stress, strain, anxiety, and futility of trying to prop up a dead guy make the movie worth watching. It's entertaining to see Richard and Larry trying to prop up a corpse. But this silly tale is sobering when we realize that God is watching as we try to prop up our old, dead lives instead of embracing and experiencing the new lives we can have because of his acceptance.

Something in us won't let go of our old lives.

The Haitian preacher spoke God's heart that night at my church, and he's speaking to you as well. "None for none" is the old, dead you. "All for all" is the new, alive you. It's the new man who heard Jesus' call to "follow me" and is now committed to finishing the journey and risk getting in the boat with him to see things he's never seen before and feel things he's never felt before in God. Just as Jesus said to those who dared to follow him when he walked along the shores of Galilee, he is saying to you now, "*Let us go over to the other side.*"[5]

Fully Identified Means Fully Defined

All-for-all people create problems for the some-for-some people.

Over the past three years, I've seen the disruptive nature of an all-for-all man colliding with some-for-some men in the life of someone in my own family—my nephew Jake. But let's be clear about one thing up front: Jake was a card-carrying none-for-none man, without God for the first twenty-two years of his life. In fact, just prior to his initial encounter with Christ, Jake was robbed in a drug deal that went bad. He was pistol-whipped, beaten, and abandoned, with no one to help him and no resources to get home. This was the context of Jake's spiritual awakening.

Now let's fast-forward.

Jake's desperation afforded no illusions about how he was rescued from self-destruction. God opened his eyes to see how much he was loved and how completely he had been forgiven and accepted in Christ. His attitude change was immediate. His

FAILSAFE

spiritual appetite was voracious. Just slap the all-for-all label on my nephew—true from the beginning and true now. So when Jake began connecting with Christian men who would rationalize attitudes and behaviors they knew were inconsistent with showing love for God or people, it confused him. A some-for-some commitment simply did not compute. His experience with Christ and his gratitude to Christ for lifting him "out of the slimy pit"[6] made the idea of excusing sin or compartmentalizing his commitment to Jesus a cheapening of God's lavish grace. His friends would say, "God understands and will forgive me" as a pretext for behavior inconsistent with their faith in Christ.

Jake believed a simple look in the Bible and a reminder of what it says would be enough to convince the some-for-some lobby to convert and join him in the all-for-all party. His attempts at this, however, were fruitless and frustrating. After months of being the "wet blanket" guy who smothered unhealthy groupthink and associated behaviors, Jake had to leave the first circle of believing friends he had ever known and set sail to find companions who would encourage, model, and support his all-for-all response to Jesus' love and acceptance. He understood fully what Jesus had done for him, and the outworking of that was that he would not dilute his commitment to gain acceptance from other men. His story is an instructive picture of what we can expect to encounter in an all-for-all journey with Christ.

Jake's journey reflects the good news that a fully accepted, fully loved, and fully identified person in Christ will be able to stand in the fires of life and emerge out of them not having compromised *anything* spiritually. That's powerful truth! The fear, the doubt, the holding on to, or the returning partially to our old patterns has been put to death and has been replaced by a new, totally loyal identity that *thrives* on the process of dying to sin and being alive to God. This is Jake. This is me. This is you. This is the place where every believer strives to be in response to Christ's love—a confident and committed place where we reflect the all-for-all kind of man Jesus was.

> [The Pharisees said to Jesus,] "Teacher . . . we know that you are a man of integrity and that you teach the way of God in accordance with the truth. You aren't swayed by others, because you pay no attention to who they are."[7]

The some-for-some religious establishment tried to sway Jesus, discourage him through pressure and intimidation, and trap and label him because he was an all-for-all man secure in God's love versus insecure like them. Jesus wasn't swayed. That's what spiritual freedom is and does. It can't be bullied into conformity. God's acceptance rises in us in front of men, just as it did with his Son.

> A voice from heaven said, "This is my Son, whom I love; with him I am well pleased."[8]

A strong moment. A strong name. A strong love. And the strongest blessing from the strongest force in the universe. But as Jesus moved from this moment and started his pilgrimage back to the Father, he lived a life, he died a death, and he came alive again on earth. His journey is our journey. His experience is our experience. Through fully identifying with that core truth, our hearts will be fully redefined and reminded of "how wide and long and high and deep is the love of Christ." We will "know this love that surpasses knowledge—that you may be filled to the measure of all the fullness of God."[9]

Being fully accepted and fully loved allows us to *fully identify* with Christ.

I Have Been Crucified with Christ

> I have been crucified with Christ and I no longer live,
> but Christ lives in me. The life I now live in the body, I
> live by faith in the Son of God, who loved me and gave
> himself for me.[10]

In the first century, a crucifixion meant that someone stopped living 100 percent of the time. Jesus stopped living physically. His physical experience now becomes our spiritual process through the presence of Christ. The great apostle Paul described how the forces that controlled him before Christ entered his life were now dead, and he considered that former man crucified. That reality reflects an exchange of leadership and control inwardly. Paul was no longer calling the shots and *couldn't call the shots* in light of Jesus' new Kingdom rule inside him. It's the same for us. We experience a spiritual death and a spiritual change of leadership. The chump (the old you) is out, and the champ (the new you in Christ) is in.

Think new rule. New filter. New energy.

> For we know that our old self was crucified with him so
> that the body ruled by sin might be done away with, that
> we should no longer be slaves to sin— because anyone
> who has died has been set free from sin.[11]

Jesus dies *for* sin. I die *to* sin.

When we have an authentic encounter with God's love, certain considerations happen immediately because our behaviors have now lost their significance. We stop chasing acceptance and doing stupid things to get it. The process is both private and public. It is seen and unseen. It is internal and external. It is also liberating on so many levels—especially at the outset of our walk with Jesus.

As on any journey, detours can arise that subtly and powerfully separate us from this truest truth about ourselves. Unplanned, long seasons of pain and loss can wear us down emotionally and make us vulnerable spiritually. There can be powerful cultural movements or, as we more recently found out, pandemics that knock us off our mark, bring out the worst from our "old self," redirect our focus, and stoke insecurity and fear. Old demons we thought were crucified are suddenly alive and beckoning us with great force under the pressures of life and the unknown. Think about it.

Have you scratched your head in confusion upon hearing news that someone you believed to be a follower of Christ has fallen into a pattern of behavior that you would never associate with that person? Or, on a more personal level, have you ever felt as if you had an out-of-body experience where you abandoned your identity in Christ in a moment of vulnerability and weakness and did the unthinkable?

This is when we must pause and account for the fragility and susceptibility of our identity in Christ. While powerful and central to our self-perception and self-regard, working out the identity God has worked into us through faith in Christ is a spiritual battle that must be fought daily and reinforced through simple spiritual disciplines. This means that fortifying but difficult lifestyle changes may be in order, like the one my nephew made. A reordering of our priorities to afford more intimate space for time in God's Word, for honest reflection, and for uninterrupted listening to God could be needed. More personally, uncomfortable but truthful conversations about random or harmful impulses we're experiencing might need to be shared with a close friend or pastor now versus later. For many men, conversations activated by the clear but convicting direction of Scripture could be God's solution for remaining in his love. For all men of faith, connecting in some form of spiritual community where there is transparency, biblical reciprocity, and welcomed accountability is a powerful context for consistency.

This is how we live in God's acceptance.

When we proactively build a lifestyle that reinforces and reaffirms our identity in Christ, we will begin to more consistently find ourselves saying no to things that harm our relationships with God and people. Why? Because with consistency comes courage. We can look in the mirror and stay there to confront the some-for-some patterns we see. We find ourselves coming back to the cross as often as we need to in order to remember, reflect on, and repent of destructive patterns of self and sin. We participate in his death so we can experience his life.

> Put to death, therefore, whatever belongs to your earthly
> nature: sexual immorality, impurity, lust, evil desires and
> greed, which is idolatry. Because of these, the wrath of
> God is coming. You used to walk in these ways, in the life
> you once lived. But now you must also rid yourselves of
> all such things as these: anger, rage, malice, slander, and
> filthy language from your lips. Do not lie to each other,
> since you have taken off your old self with its practices
> and have put on the new self, which is being renewed in
> knowledge in the image of its Creator.[12]

Jesus dies; I die. That defines me, and it is my new identity.

I Have Been Resurrected with Christ

> We were therefore buried with him through baptism
> into death in order that, just as Christ was raised from
> the dead through the glory of the Father, we too may
> live a new life.

For if we have been united with him in a death
like his, we will certainly also be united with him in a
resurrection like his. . . .
      The death he died, he died to sin once for all; but the
life he lives, he lives to God.
      In the same way, count yourselves dead to sin but
alive to God in Christ Jesus. Therefore do not let sin
reign in your mortal body so that you obey its evil desires.
Do not offer any part of yourself to sin as an instrument
of wickedness, but rather offer yourselves to God as
those who have been brought from death to life; and
offer every part of yourself to him as an instrument of
righteousness.[13]

Being united with Christ means living *like him in the present
moment.* Our no to sin is always a yes to God. We aren't just dead
to sin; we are alive to God on the inside, eager and excited to live
God's way. What does being alive to God feel like?

- We are confident in saying no to temptation because it is
  a yes to God's plan.
- We have courage to say no to ourselves because it means
  we can say yes to others.
- We have the inner conviction to go *against* the pressure of
  culture in order to be *for* Christ.
- We increasingly see the benefit of pausing and reconsidering
  our way so we can seek out and pursue *God's way.*

Being fully identified with Christ would be a bummer if all we
did was say no to things. You might be holy, but man, would you
be boring! God's love is a powerful force not just for restraining sin
but also for releasing and replacing it with his will in real time, in

real spaces, and in real people's lives. That's exciting. Being resurrected with Christ feels like an adventure, thanks to God's love. For certain, to feel fully alive, something needs to stop. But that isn't the end of the journey; it's just the beginning. Something also needs to start and continue forward to finish the story!

> Because of his great love for us, God, who is rich in mercy, made us alive with Christ even when we were dead in transgressions—it is by grace you have been saved.[14]

Jesus is alive; I'm alive. That defines me, and it is my new identity.

I Have Been Seated with Christ

> God raised us up with Christ and seated us with him in the heavenly realms in Christ Jesus, in order that in the coming ages he might show the incomparable riches of his grace, expressed in his kindness to us in Christ Jesus.[15]

It's generous when someone gives you the best seat in the house as a gift. In my years as a pastor, good friends and acquaintances who know my passion for sports and sporting events have blessed me with some amazing seats that I could never have personally afforded. Sometimes it has been jaw dropping. To be able to enjoy a Major League Baseball game or a National Football League game from a skybox can't be beat. That vantage point allows you to participate in the action, and the food is amazing! The bottom line about great seats is this: *the better the seats, the better the experience.* As believers fully identified with Christ, we have been given access and authority to participate in this life from Christ's seat.

At the moment, we cannot take our seat with Christ physically, but that doesn't limit us at all spiritually.

> Since, then, you have been raised with Christ, set your hearts on things above, where Christ is, seated at the right hand of God. Set your minds on things above, not on earthly things. For you died, and your life is now hidden with Christ in God. When Christ, who is your life, appears, then you also will appear with him in glory.[16]

> For through him we both have access to the Father by one Spirit. Consequently, you are no longer foreigners and strangers, but fellow citizens with God's people and also members of his household.[17]

> Let us then approach God's throne of grace with confidence, so that we may receive mercy and find grace to help us in our time of need.[18]

Prayer punches your all-access ticket. Faith in God's words seats you with Christ. Conversion sets new things in motion. The Holy Spirit animates and makes tangible the results. In other words, the future "then and there" of heaven is actually the present "here and now" on earth. Eternal life doesn't begin when our hearts stop. Eternal life started the moment we received the person and work of Christ, and it's in full force right now! That is why God's Word is emphatic and consistent: God wants us to practice the life of heaven here on earth, and that includes coming confidently to him and claiming our seat with Christ as members of God's household.

All privileges. All access. All authority.

Will we fight for it? Will we battle for his love to manifest itself fully in us? There must be a moment when we reflect on all we are and all we are presently doing and then say to ourselves,

> I once thought these things were valuable, but now I consider them worthless because of what Christ has done. Yes, everything else is worthless when compared with the infinite value of knowing Christ Jesus my Lord. For his sake I have discarded everything else, counting it all as garbage, so that I could gain Christ and become one with him. I no longer count on my own righteousness through obeying the law; rather, I become righteous through faith in Christ. For God's way of making us right with himself depends on faith. I want to know Christ and experience the mighty power that raised him from the dead. I want to suffer with him, sharing in his death, so that one way or another I will experience the resurrection from the dead!
>
> I don't mean to say that I have already achieved these things or that I have already reached perfection. But I press on to possess that perfection for which Christ Jesus first possessed me.[19]

Pressing deep. Knowing him deeper. Experiencing him deeply.

Every man who professes faith in Christ wants to possess on the inside that perfect love *"for which Christ Jesus first possessed me."* We want what Jesus came to win for us spiritually, and we want to see it fully accomplished in our lives! It's not necessary to know exactly what that looks like, but we do know the direction we need to take: putting sin to death like Jesus did, becoming more alive to God's purposes like Jesus, and consistently accessing our heavenly position in Jesus. This is what God wants for us—the fullest inner connection possible, and the comfort that connection brings into our lives. But do we want it enough to risk spiritually for it?

It's impossible to please God apart from faith. And why? Because anyone who wants to approach God must believe both that he exists and that he cares enough to respond to those who seek him.[20]

Do you believe that God cares enough to respond in this moment? Then risk it.

Jesus,

I want to fight for your fullest life to be manifested in me. I am going to take my stand for it right now based on who you are. I am not going to let anything keep me from the life your love has provided and the inner works your love wants to accomplish in me. Jesus, your life is the one I want to fully identify and align with. I will not prop up the old me any longer or make excuses for old ways being part of my new life in you. God has declared that person dead. I declare now in faith that I am crucified with Christ, and it is no longer I who live but you who are going to live in and through me. I consider myself dead to all forms of sin but alive to God. I accept my position in Christ—seated with you—and will access heaven as much as possible as I live out my time on earth. This is the life you want for me, and this is the life I need your power to help me live. Fill me with the Holy Spirit so that I can work with you each day to choose this life, this love, and this leading now and forever. Amen.

BEING SECURE

4

FIERCELY COMFORTABLE

The Inner Change

THE VIDEO CLIP is called "Toddler's Tantrum after Missed Putt." Look it up for fun. It's only forty-eight seconds long, but it's an action-packed sequence that does not disappoint. A little toddler named Peter is standing over a four-inch gimme putt, the kind you simply give to a fellow golfer because the ball is so close to the hole that ninety-nine times out of a hundred, it will go in. Holding his oversize plastic golf club in his hands, Peter draws it back slowly and brings it forward to make contact and sink his putt. Clearly he expects the ball to go in the hole, but in a cruel twist of fate, it goes in a little and then "lips out." In then out. So close and yet so far. Hope and then despair. Or, in little Peter's case, expectation, hope, dismay, and meltdown.

There is no failsafe.

The ball lips out. Peter's two-year-old mind processes the

unfathomable. His brain and body then begin what is known in neuroscience as a *stress response*. I've studied this process in men quite a bit. It's just funnier watching a two-year-old cycle through it! After Peter's amygdala sends a distress signal, the hypothalamus activates the sympathetic nervous system by sending signals through the autonomic nerves to the adrenal glands. As a result of that communication, epinephrine is pumped into the bloodstream of little Peter's body. All of this takes about 1.5 seconds. What follows is a sustained response known to you and me as a temper tantrum, which has both common and unique characteristics. This tantrum was so good, more than four million people around the world saw it shortly after it happened.

It's cute. It's expected with toddlers. It's called the "terrible twos" for a reason.

Little Peter will grow up and grow out of it, right?

The world hopes so.

Inner Man versus Inner Boy

The expressed hope of growing up is confirmed in the Bible.

> When I was a child, I talked like a child, I thought like a child, I reasoned like a child. When I became a man, I put the ways of childhood behind me.[1]

I love that these words were written by one of the most spiritually mature men to ever follow Jesus. The apostle Paul is saying to every man that we are all on the same journey, and that spiritual and emotional maturity is a battle of *ways*. If you're like me, there are parts of you that you feel are really grown up, and then, under the right circumstances and the right types of pressure, there are parts of you (maturity-wise) that reflect a junior high school mentality and response. Welcome to the battle of ways—the inner boy fighting to prevent the inner man from rising.

Wearing our spiritual "big-boy pants" requires living in God's acceptance.

It means not being easily discouraged, withdrawing from people, or throwing an adult temper tantrum that makes everyone around us miserable or suffer. God's acceptance gives peace, confidence, and assurance to the inner boy in the rearview mirror. Our foundation of inner security through God's acceptance is strong and allows us to risk new emotional growth and maturity in a *masculine context*. Think about it this way: For every way of living as a man, God has a way of being a man rooted in our identity in Christ.

How we relate to ourselves, women, children, friends, and humanity as men is modeled in Christ, and his example gives us a direction we can trust. How we respond to and process conflict as men is transformed through inner security. Disengagement and bottling up our emotions give way to working things out and risking dialogue. How we pursue emotional and sexual intimacy doesn't need to reside in an alternative life of fantasy. Through God's love, we can achieve *real intimacy* through new maturity and learning how to love sacrificially. Even how we relate to other men can radically change because of the securing power of God's love. When we know that God is present and has our back in this life and eternally, we can stop competing with other men and start connecting meaningfully and deeply.

This is the life we're after as men of God. This is the way we want to be. This is what we're asking God to accomplish through his acceptance of us. This is our constant direction in our personal prayers: that we grow inwardly more like Christ.

[I pray] that He would grant you, according to the riches of His glory, to be strengthened with power through His

Spirit in the *inner man*, so that Christ may dwell in your hearts through faith; and that you [would be] rooted and grounded in love.[2]

When God's love is in control, he will direct us to pursue lifestyles that reflect to the world the strength, character, and emotional maturity of Christ himself. Wherever you are right now in your journey, this "work" in you is ongoing and won't stop until your heart stops. I know that's an uncomfortable thought, especially for all of the top performers who want to summit the mountain, plant the flag, and declare territory conquered. But when the mountain is Christlikeness on the inside—the inner man complete—you are never done becoming like Jesus until you are actually with him. In fact, that is why you're holding this book in your hands and this conversation is happening! I need to grow up into him in every way, and I'm not supposed to go it alone. You are coming with me! God has goals for our connection, our journeys, and our transformations.

Listen with your spirit to what he is doing in this moment:

He handed out gifts of apostle, prophet, evangelist, and pastor-teacher to train Christ's followers in skilled servant work, working within Christ's body, the church, until we're all moving rhythmically and easily with each other, efficient and graceful in response to God's Son, fully mature adults, fully developed within and without, fully alive like Christ.

No prolonged infancies among us, please. We'll not tolerate babes in the woods, small children who are an easy mark for impostors. God wants us to grow up, to know the whole truth and tell it in love—like Christ in everything. We take our lead from Christ, who is the source of everything we do. He keeps us in step with each other. His very breath and blood flow through us, nourishing us so that we will grow up healthy in God, robust in love.[3]

Did you see yourself in that description? You are a highly skilled servant. You are becoming fully mature in Christ "within and without." God has decided that you are getting some new big-boy pants that you'll wear proudly and well. In fact, after this is done, you're going to look "like Christ in everything." But you need a source for the growth God is planning. You need to keep up. You need to follow Jesus closely. You need to breathe him in and feel his blood start to flow through your inner man, nourishing your maturity and growing you up.

Healthy in God. Robust in love.

A man.

Fierce and Free

No man tells stories to other men about how he played it safe. But every man loves to tell and retell stories of the risks he took.

The men on the shores of Galilee who did not get into the boat with Jesus ended their stories at the shore. In contrast, we're still telling and retelling the stories of the men who got into the boat and saw major miracles, raw power, and victories over nature, evil, scarcity, depletion, and disease. In their minds, the value of the opportunity outweighed the potential risks involved. In the end, it turned ordinary men into fiercely focused warriors, free to risk it all, including death for eleven of the twelve disciples.

A willingness to risk it all is at the center of a relationship with Christ. He valued us, and that made Jesus fierce in his pursuit and willing to suffer freely. To him, we were worth it. He laid hold of us, and now that same fierceness is being reproduced in us, and we are laying hold of him. His love is making us fierce because we value his approval and acceptance above all. His unconditional and inseparable love will also break the chains of past patterns in our lives so we can set sail in the direction of personal change— sometimes at great personal cost. We have a cause to die for— literally and figuratively. That cause is Christ and his likeness being formed in us. The greatest threat to evil in this world is men who have been made fierce as we become inwardly secure and singular in our identity in Christ.

It makes me think of John at my church. He has been cleaning pools for the past twenty years in south Orange County. As regular and familiar as his job had become over that time, it was a mirror for his faith journey. Routine had replaced a once robust and exciting relationship with God. You could say that John's faith was dormant—there but not active, not public, and not a threat to evil. That was until my friend Jim DeFord saw John cleaning his pool, and God prompted Jim to get to know his pool guy. A few conversations into this process, Jim discovered that John believed in Christ, and he began encouraging John to move from being affiliated with Jesus in name only to being activated for Jesus in a way consistent with his identity in Christ. As steps in this direc- tion, Jim encouraged John to come to church with him on Sunday and to men's community gatherings during the week. John never could have anticipated the life-altering consequences that would come when he accepted Jim's invitation to action.

At Sunday service John heard the words, "The truest thing about you is what God says is true." At men's study he heard the proclamation, "You are made by God, made for God, loved by God, and going back to God." Each time John showed up at church, a fresh wind began to blow on those initial embers of con- versation. What was once ambivalence became an out-of-control wildfire of purpose, consuming every dimension of John's life. He was coming into an awareness of who he was as a son of God, and that identity, combined with the inner security that flowed from it, began working its way out of him. John was no longer only affiliated with Jesus; he was *activated for Jesus* through his identity in Christ. He was experiencing the promise of life in Christ, and others were witnessing it—especially his wife, who, after experiencing firsthand John's new maturity and consistency, tore up the divorce papers she had been begging him to sign.

This process is like watching a superhero being born! Men discover an identity that is dangerous *and* good. You can tell it's coming from a deep place within a man versus being propped up by outer appearances or image. Men know who they ultimately are in God, which gives them new confidence, new freedom, and new purpose in this life. In their new identity, they have been given special power through the Holy Spirit to say and do things that bring God's love and justice. They are commissioned to defend the defenseless and bring compassion in various forms to all people instead of only some. They can, in a God-approved way, stick it to the evil one and effectively thwart his destructive intentions through personal presence and action. That ethos of being great and doing great things is planted in men by God and can be engaged in real time (versus fantasy) through a relationship with Jesus, the Son of God and the Man who brings love *and* justice.

John has become almost unstoppable. He lives as if he has nothing to lose and today could be his last. Every day and every moment count. He knows and believes that he is going to be okay no matter what. He is under no illusions about the sacrifices he is being called to make in his identity. In fact, in a counterintuitive and positive reframing of hardship, he knows that God is using "all things" to make him like Jesus. This new mindset and process reflect a new understanding—a powerful one. John is spiritually and emotionally secure in God's love and purpose for his life.

> And we know that in all things God works for the good
> of those who love him, who have been called according to
> his purpose. For those God foreknew he also predestined
> to be conformed to the image of his Son, that he might
> be the firstborn among many brothers and sisters.[4]

Key words? *We know.* John knows. Do you know?

In no area of the human experience is such confidence more desperately needed than in the area of our emotional security. Every human being ever created has been emotionally constructed to have a self-concept and self-worth rooted in the fact that we are made by God, loved by God, and made for God. This emotional foundation, built into our existence, is the only framework that gives us internal and *eternal* stability, provides tangible comfort, assigns indestructible worth, and infuses every dimension and process of life with purpose. We *know it* only through Christ, and when we come to *know it* experientially and not just intellectually, it provides what all human beings are desperate for emotionally—comfort.

> Therefore if you have any encouragement from being
> united with Christ, if any comfort from his love, if any
> common sharing in the Spirit, if any tenderness and
> compassion, then make my joy complete by being
> like-minded, having the same love, being one in spirit
> and of one mind.[5]

Encouragement. Comfort. Intimacy. Tenderness. Compassion. That's what God's love delivers. That's what it does. It sets us free. "So if the Son sets you free, you will be free indeed."[6]

Free to do what, exactly? Think about John from my church. Free to leave one way of being for God's way of being. We can face the stale parts of us and desire the fresh. We can grow up and grow out of old patterns. Becoming like Jesus is worth any risk to our egos, our image, or our reputations. His love makes us fiercely comfortable with the process. His presence with us in the process sets us free to go for big victories and slay long-standing foes that have kept us insecure and immature. He's got us and is never leaving our side. So it's time to stop living out of what we lack and start living out of what God has provided through Christ as newer, Spirit-filled, mature, and complete men. This is the man you've always wanted to be, and the man everyone in your life is waiting to see and embrace. This is the man evil now must account for—one not ruled by silly insecurities and fears but filled with the confidence God has supplied.

Goodbye shoreline. Hello open seas and new adventures in change.

> It is obvious what kind of life develops out of trying to get your own way all the time: repetitive, loveless, cheap sex; a stinking accumulation of mental and emotional garbage; frenzied and joyless grabs for happiness; trinket gods; magic-show religion; paranoid loneliness; cutthroat competition; all-consuming-yet-never-satisfied wants; a brutal temper; an impotence to love or be loved; divided homes and divided lives; small-minded and lopsided pursuits; the vicious habit of depersonalizing everyone into a rival; uncontrolled and uncontrollable addictions; ugly parodies of community. I could go on.
>
> This isn't the first time I have warned you, you know. If you use your freedom this way, you will not inherit God's kingdom.

But what happens when we live God's way? He brings gifts into our lives, much the same way that fruit appears in an orchard—things like affection for others, exuberance about life, serenity. We develop a willingness to stick with things, a sense of compassion in the heart, and a conviction that a basic holiness permeates things and people. We find ourselves involved in loyal commitments, not needing to force our way in life, able to marshal and direct our energies wisely.[7]

We all make choices. Fear moves us to choose self-protection, self-importance, self-gratification, and self-preservation—take your pick. We act, reason, and think like children, and yet we are grown men! Sacrificial love, by contrast, makes us stop and reflect on the choices we've been making. God's acceptance renders useless our broken quests for visibility and attention. Christ's action for us compels us to choose a new way to be and believe, which leads to new behaviors. God's love locks us down inside; as a result, we become fiercely comfortable with who we are in his love. That security frees us up to make some radical and risky choices to change our ways.

Now we look inside, and what we see is that anyone united with the Messiah gets a fresh start, is created new. The old life is gone; a new life burgeons! Look at it! All this comes from the God who settled the relationship between us and him, and then called us to settle our relationships with each other.[8]

Did you hear that? It's settled.

Deep Love, Deeper Works

Fear makes bad men from the inside out. Love makes good men from the inside out. That's the war we find ourselves in. Fear keeps us immature. When love defeats fear, we can start the maturing process. But not until then. That process requires *knowledge* of God's love becoming an actual *work* of God's love inside us. The only way to accomplish that journey is to continuously pour the truth about his love into our minds, hearts, and souls until it becomes our strength. Think about how marination changes the nature of food. The more the raw meat soaks in a marinade, the more it takes on the character of whatever constitutes that marinade. My ribs, for example, go into the marinade without anything influencing the character of the meat. But the longer I soak the meat—many times overnight—the more deeply its nature changes. When those ribs hit the grill after soaking, they aren't simply ribs anymore because of my process. They are an experience! They are fundamentally changed.

Think of the Bible—God's Word—as the dominant ingredient in your mental marinade. God's love for humanity pervades God's Word. It is the dominant message. As you soak in his Word daily, meditate on that truth, and think deeply about its implications, you internalize God's love for you. As a consequence, your self-perception is permanently and fundamentally altered. In fact, this book is part of that marinating and meditating process, but ultimately the steady and daily consumption of God's truest truth about you—that he fully accepts and loves you—will fundamentally alter your self-perception and self-regard, which will transform your life into a new experience.

As you marinate in the Bible regularly and process what it says intellectually and emotionally, the deeper works begin to manifest themselves. These works occur by grace alone through faith alone in Christ alone. In other words, if we *choose* to let God's love cover us, define us, fill us, free us, and transform our ways of thinking, he promises to transform our ways of living. You can pray them. You can speak them. But most of all, God desires that you receive them into your spirit and let them define you.

The Truest Truths about the New You

Gone is shame. God has replaced it with dignity and worth. This means I can stop listening to the lies that diminish who I am and start allowing God's love to tell me who I am—his creative work, valued and worth dying for. This means all things are possible, and I possess a future that is different from my past. I receive his deepest love into me so that his deepest works can be accomplished in and through me.

Gone is anxiety over my worth. It has been replaced with peace and assurance through Christ in me. I can stop trying to prove my value before people, making decisions to please them, and I can start living out of God's acceptance of me. I am free from comparisons. I am settled because he has settled the issue of worth. I have nothing to prove. I am complete in Christ. I receive his peace, which comes from being a child of God.

Gone are bitterness and anger over my losses. They have been replaced with love and compassion through Christ in me. I can stop projecting my anger onto others now. I am loved perfectly and sacrificially by Christ. I am forgiven perfectly and compassionately by Christ. I can now love and forgive those who have hurt me and those God has called me to love. I receive his kindness through the Holy Spirit inside of me.

Gone are sadness and despair from events I could not control. Joy and hope have replaced those negative feelings through the risen Christ in me. He will redeem my losses in this life or the next as promised. If he can use the death of Christ to redeem me, he can redeem every negative event connected to my life. What people intended for evil, God will redeem for good.[9] My circumstances do not define me, because God is using them to grow me and make me like Christ. He is at work, and I am seeking his good purpose in everything. I receive the joy and hope of his redeeming Spirit.

Gone are the impatience and irritation that make me and others frustrated. Those have been replaced by patience and long-suffering through Christ in me. I can stop being in a hurry, and I can start being present with God and people. I can stop complaining when things don't happen when or how I want them to happen. God is in charge, and he loves me and knows what is best for me. God's Word, his Spirit, and people are never an interruption. God himself left the comfort of heaven and the fellowship of the Godhead to redeem me, and because of that experience, I am compelled to reproduce it. Now, as God has assigned worth and value to me, all the people he has placed in my life qualify as recipients of my sacrifice, time, initiative, and patience. I receive the patience of Christ through the Holy Spirit in me.

Gone are selfishness and indifference. Kindness and generosity have replaced them through Christ in me. It is his kindness and generosity toward me when I least deserved them that give me a future and forgiveness forever. Whatever I am and have that is good comes from him. It isn't mine. He met me in my need generously. He bestowed amazing grace upon me. He raised me up. He heard my cry. My God is generous with his blessing. I receive his kind and generous Spirit so that I can bless others as he has blessed me.

Gone are harshness and hardness from my spirit. So many times, our ability to wound another human being has nothing to do with what's visible. It's not about what we see or even what someone did. It emanates from a place inside us that houses the toxic emotions connected to other formational and harmful encounters in our past that lurk in our emotions and get triggered. Much as an oil deposit is tapped unintentionally and spews forth its dark and messy substance, human beings can be tapped and spew toxic emotions onto others, who had no intention of bringing out what was inside. By leaving it unaddressed, people can become what I call "emotional porcupines." Don't attempt to hug one when their quills are up, because you'll walk out of the encounter in pain.

The Bible describes our encounter with God as a healing encounter with divine kindness. This experience, when understood emotionally and accepted personally, has the power to transform toxic emotions within us into new spiritual abilities and strengths for the edification of others. Specifically, hardness of spirit and harshness of soul are exchanged for gentleness and tenderness through Christ in me. When I deserved judgment, he showed me mercy. Jesus was tender with me because he is gentle and humble in heart and gives me rest.[10] I don't have to demand things now. I don't have to carry around pressures and take them out on others. I have Christ who carries my burdens so I can stay lighter inside and make life lighter for others instead of heavier. As a man in community with others, I receive the gentleness and tenderness of the Holy Spirit so I can lift others up and ease their burdens.

Gone are selfish ways of thinking and living. The part of me that takes versus gives has been replaced with the good and giving Spirit of Christ. By Christ's power and in his name, I am a child of God who can always say no to myself in order to say yes to loving God and people wherever I am and whatever I'm doing. Good things come out of the good man because of the good that is in him.[11] Jesus is good. Jesus is doing good. He lives in me. He is the good I will let out into the world. In faith I'm going to give him my body, my energy, and all my abilities so he can use them to do good through me. I receive his goodness through the Holy Spirit.

Gone is the unfaithful, untrustworthy, and irresponsible man. I am now a faithful man though Christ. Jesus was faithful to the end on earth for me. I will be faithful in loving his ways and loving people on earth. Christ is available and reliable and has never been unfaithful to his promises. Christ is the definition of integrity. He lives in me, and I receive his faithfulness through the Holy Spirit.

Gone are impulsiveness and immature self-indulgence. These have been replaced by self-control, restraint, and discipline through Christ in me. Jesus knew why he came to earth: to complete the mission God had given him. God has an intention, purpose, mission, and work for me now. I will define my yeses and nos around his Word and his ways. I will listen to the Spirit's voice promptly and consistently when he tells me to show love for God and people. I receive the self-control of the Holy Spirit through Christ.

These declarations are works of God, and his aim is to complete them in you.

> There has never been the slightest doubt in my mind that
> the God who started this great work in you would keep
> at it and bring it to a flourishing finish on the very day
> Christ Jesus appears.[12]

Deeper works can now begin *because* you are deeply loved.

> Is there no one who can do anything for me? Isn't that the
> real question?
>   The answer, thank God, is that Jesus Christ can
> and does. He acted to set things right in this life of
> contradictions where I want to serve God with all my
> heart and mind, but am pulled by the influence of sin to
> do something totally different.

With the arrival of Jesus, the Messiah, that fateful dilemma is resolved. Those who enter into Christ's being-here-for-us no longer have to live under a continuous, low-lying black cloud. A new power is in operation. The Spirit of life in Christ, like a strong wind, has magnificently cleared the air, freeing you from a fated lifetime of brutal tyranny at the hands of sin and death.[13]

You are a man who is fierce in Christ. A man who is free in him. A man the world is waiting for.

Jesus,

Thank you for being my model of strength and love. There is no doubt in my mind that I want to be more like you—the kind of man those around me can look to and rely on the way I look to and rely on you. But I can't accomplish that on my own. The only way to do that is through your strong love for me and the encouragement to risk radical change. Help me to risk great change through you, in you, and for you. Today I reject the immaturity that comes from fear and self-protection, and I declare a new commitment to your calling for greater maturity in Christ. Jesus, thank you for calling me into your character, providing me with your power, and supporting me on this journey with the solid foundation of your love. I want to be fiercely comfortable saying no to myself and yes to your desired changes in my life. Grant me now the fruit of the Holy Spirit I need the most to honor you and love others. Amen.

5

SECURITY THREATS

The Inner Challenge

BIG EVIL LOVES BIG DATA. Pull together the data security officers for Facebook, Wells Fargo, Target, Marriott, and Capital One and ask them how the past few years have been with respect to losing company records. The numbers are stunning. In 2019, the worst year ever for security breaches, corporations large and small suffered more than 7,098 data breaches exposing 15.1 billion personal records of their clients, customers, and users.[1] That's roughly double the number of total human beings on planet earth! Keep in mind that this doesn't include the 7.2 billion malware attacks and 152 million ransomware attacks during the first nine months of the same time period.[2] For each individual number that rolls up into these astronomical metanumbers, there is a real person who has become exploitable financially and, together with other victims, loses between $15 and $20 billion annually.

I happen to be one of those numbers. A person successfully stole my identity.

It was a day like any other. I got to work, opened my laptop, and then launched my email program. Lots of new messages, one of which was an email from the comptroller of our organization. Right away the tone was off. The subject line simply read *INVOICE*. The message in her forwarded email was direct and to the point: "Why didn't you discuss this with me when we met this week? See below."

When I scrolled down, I saw a message *from me* directing her to pay an invoice for sixteen thousand dollars to a consultant. Asking her to pay invoices is not an unfamiliar occurrence, but three red flags went up. The first? *I never wrote this message.* The second? The words used in the email—distant and demanding—were also not me. Whoever wrote it was trying to create urgency through intimidation and power language, which is not my style. The person impersonating me blew it there. The third red flag? The amount! The hacker who was phishing for dollars mistakenly concluded that this was a typical fee for a consultant to charge a nonprofit organization for services rendered. Wow. That "consultant" must have been reeeaaalllly good! It was an active takeover of my personal identity, my position, my authority, and my character in real time and in really *dangerous* ways.

Those red flags created a red alert.

I quickly scrolled through my contacts, reached out to a friend who happens to be a cybersecurity expert, and told him what had happened. Immediately he locked everything down for me and explained *how* and *where* this impersonator gained access to my system, took over my identity, and started manipulating my life. A few hours later, he called me back and said, "The hacker is now trying to break into the RSS feed again. Do you want to see him trying?"

"One hundred percent" was my reply.

So I gave my friend permission to take over control of my computer, open windows, and walk me through several security layers in the system until we landed at a crime in progress.

He said, "There he or she is."

The hacker's presence was evident as I watched someone typing letters and symbols, erasing those same letters and symbols, and then retyping new letters and symbols. The hacker was trying to "pick the lock," and it was clear that what worked in the past was now not working because of the new security measures that had been installed. It was the weirdest feeling watching someone trying to destroy my life. This criminal was locked out of my system, but what amazed me was the persistence and belief that it was still possible to get in. Stubbornly and repetitively, this person would type new letters and symbols, erase them, and start over. Again and again and again. In my case, the cybersecurity people were able to track the hacker's IP address to somewhere in the metro London area 5,400 miles away. That was another odd feeling—this was happening remotely from some residence or coffee shop across the Atlantic, and no one there had any idea what was happening. All over the world, targeted evil is present, active, and working to divest us of the livelihoods we work so hard for.

The subtlety and sophistication of the attacks are what make them so effective. Cyberattacks are designed to create fear. Government impostors saying you are violating some law, tech-support scams saying your system is vulnerable to hackers, or business-associate manipulations where it appears you are the one making a request. All of these cybersecurity threats are lurking dangers that can exploit vulnerabilities and steal what is essential to living.

Eventually the hacker gave up after realizing it was no longer possible to break into my system and take over my identity. The whole experience changed my attitude toward identity theft and cybercrime. In addition to installing some protective systems on my computer that would create impenetrable barriers to frustrate potential intruders, there was also a superpractical, low-tech process that would ensure no one besides the real me could log on to my computer.

It's called *two-factor identification* or *double authentication*.

You might be nodding your head right now because you have this process in place, but for those unfamiliar with it, it's exactly what it sounds like. First, you enter your username and password. Then, instead of gaining access right away, you have to give a second piece of personal information. This second factor comes from a unique source—your life! It could be something only you know—an answer to a secret question, for example. It could be something you have—like a credit card or a smartphone. It could be some unique identifying feature—like your voice or a fingerprint. The extra layer of protection and the additional actions assure me it's me! No one can log on to my computer without my being aware of it.

We take active measures when an active threat is recognized.

And just as we take action to prevent cybercriminals from gaining access to what security experts call *personally identifiable information* (PII), such as Social Security numbers, credit-card numbers, or bank-account passwords vital to daily life, the same is true for believers in Christ when it comes to protecting ourselves spiritually and emotionally from the master hacker, Satan. The fact that God fully accepts, fully loves, and fully defines us changes everything. These truths are the personally identifiable information that Satan values and attacks the most using fear.

These attacks involve suggestions that, somehow, God's love and care for you are limited in some aspect of your life, and that you are losing out, missing out, or striking out by trusting in his presence and loving plan. The headline is *DON'T TRUST GOD!* Instead, you need to trust in yourself, your ways, and your plans *to win back what God cannot or will not provide for you right now.*

The suggested solution? Take God's place.

It's called *idolatry*. Move over, God!

Here's how the "solution" plays out:

- You aren't visible enough? Make yourself more visible.
- You aren't respected enough? Make others look up to you.
- You aren't successful enough? Make others work harder for you.
- You aren't wealthy enough? Take the get-rich-quick approach.
- You aren't loved enough? Find intimacy outside your marriage.
- You are missing out? Compartmentalize your faith one time and go for it!
- You aren't engaged enough? Increase your social media presence.
- You don't look the part? Fix that! Isn't that what credit cards are for?
- You feel as if life is passing you by? You only live once. Stop being so religious and stale! Live a little.
- You look like you've plateaued? Embellish things a little. Pad the numbers or the story.
- You aren't performing? Hide behind God.
- You don't want to feel like a failure? Minimize accountability and delay facing reality.
- You aren't appreciated enough? Seek out your fans, and mute your friends.

If any of these reflect how you feel, make no mistake, the hacker is present. It's subtle, but he is breaking into your mind, heart, and soul and infecting them with some nice-sounding, reasonable *suggestions*. They may seem like the right thing to do at the moment to resolve your insecurities. If successful, *you* will replace God, stop living out of his love, and start living out of fear.

> There is a way which seems right to a man,
> But its end is the way of death.[3]

Major red flag.

Red Flags

By the time we see a red flag, it often means that the root problem has been operating under the surface for some time.

When a cybercriminal has broken into your computer system or network, there are indicators that something foreign is interfering with your system's performance. You see the red flags, but they are only letting you know that some "thing" exists behind them that is causing a problem. Unfamiliar things appear. Your identity is taken over. The system is acting oddly. It's slow to respond. Manipulation is happening.

Sad to say, but all of those red flags have been true of me at one time or another in my spiritual journey with God and people. My inner man was corrupted. I believed a lie about myself, a circumstance, or a person that made me fear that God had lost control somehow and didn't care. So I decided to step in. But when I did, fear took over. I started to act oddly, taking actions that others sensed were out of character. When people asked if something was up, I was slow to recognize my dysfunctional actions. Unfamiliar and self-protective patterns emerged. Sometimes I couldn't explain my actions. I took the bait and did whatever it took to resolve the fear inside me, even if it meant sinning directly or indirectly against God or people. I confess that fear and insecurity corrupted my inner man, and since I'm sharing a cup of honesty with you, my guess is that somewhere along your journey, you've been corrupted as well.

Am I right?

Fear is a universal force that creates common responses and behaviors. The goal now is to proactively *recognize and neutralize* fear-based attacks before they damage our most important relationships.

Raise your threat level if you see or sense any of the following warning signs in yourself or someone else.

You Worry about Everything or One Thing Constantly

This is the easiest red flag to dismiss because everybody worries about something, right? Being concerned about an issue, a person, or a situation doesn't mean your inner security in God's love is compromised. That's normal and goes with the ups and downs of life and relationships. However, if you're the kind of person who worries about *everything* because you aren't sure events will safely unfold in your favor, that is a red flag. Abiding anxiety and constant worry are signals that the future (in your mind) needs to be under your control. Anxious feelings reflect the fact that your shoulders are simply not big enough to *take on the future*, and that reality gets worked out in your heart, emotions, body, and behaviors.

People also worry over a singular source of injury, loss, or pain recurring in their lives. It's not that *everything* worries you, because "everything" didn't traumatize you. But a single event or season of your life definitely did, and you worry consciously or subconsciously that it will happen again. Both kinds of worry or fear have the power to take over your perception of reality and control your behavior in subtle and powerful ways that sabotage your relationships with God, yourself, and others. When that happens, it creates patterns of deep disappointment, struggle, and fragmentation within those three critical dimensions of your life. The lie is that God's love and power can handle a lot of things, and it's good for a lot of things, just not this *one* thing. Therefore, you need to take over and calm the fear yourself.

Watch out for that evil suggestion. If you don't, the following happens.

You Are Never Safe Enough or Settled Enough

Restlessness characterizes your life. You can't get comfortable. Something has to "happen," but naming it would be too embarrassing—or it's too elusive to name. You long for comfort and constancy, but you live in a state of "temporary" with everyone and everything. So often the events and experiences of the past pollute your sense of confidence in God's love and sovereignty to the point where you feel as if all aspects of your life are in jeopardy. It then becomes hard to get close to or attach to any one thing. With that root fear in play, you consciously and subconsciously move to preempt the pain by ending things first. Fear's solution for restlessness is to pursue the next thing. Things will either end or be taken away prematurely and painfully.

The idea that "this is going to end poorly like so many things do" is a planned intrusion of your inner man, orchestrated by the master hacker, Satan. Watch out for that suggestion, because it will become a self-fulfilling prophecy if you believe it.

If you find yourself unsettled, anxious, and always wondering what is going to happen next, a gratitude inventory is in order. This means finding space to be alone, away from digital interruptions, notifications, and alerts. Next, let yourself think about all the good things God has given you, and write them down. There is no time limit for this exercise, and there will be bursts as well as lulls. The important thing is that you reflect on what you have, whom you are in relationship with, and what you feel grateful for today. As you discover gratitude and express it on paper, a mysterious and wonderful thing begins to emerge. Contentment and peace make a comeback in your life.

Do you have room in your life for more of those?

You Push and Pull in Relationships

When fear and insecurity take control, you act like you don't need someone you say is very important to you. Time passes. Conclusions are made about the relationship; it appears you are fine going it alone. But then, in a one-hundred-eighty-degree turn, you make the other person feel mission critical to your existence. In a flood of love, you privately and publicly express how much you value, need, and appreciate this person. What? That makes things doubly confusing. More time passes. Then, just when you feel close again, some fear ignites within you, you feel insecure about the relationship, and you start pushing away. You act as if you don't need the person anymore—or, worse, that you never did.

You're like an oscillating fan that hits its range limit and then turns in the other direction again and again. The only problem is that it cools nothing off! A deep fear of being abandoned or rejected produces this dynamic of pushing away the people you really want closest to you. Then, once others separate from you or walk away, you energetically and emotionally tell them you need them and can't do life without them. *The belief that people are both needed and a threat to you is dysfunctional.* Big red flag.

More importantly, that kind of thinking has subversive power over you and your relationships. When that happens, vacillating relationship cycles ensue, creating patterns of deep disappointment, struggle, and fragmentation within those three relational dimensions of your life.

You Hate Conflict of Any Kind and Find Yourself Accommodating or Apologizing a Lot

When fear and insecurity take control, you are never sure of how you're coming across to others. This insecurity births the feeling that you're always doing something wrong and then having to apologize for it. The odd thing about this is that you behave apologetically even if you've done nothing to harm anyone in any way. I call these "just in case" apologies that cover all the bases. You apologize just in case you did something, or might have done something. The idea is this: The fear of someone being angry or upset with you is so unacceptable at a deep level that you move to preempt even the possibility by always accommodating people or banking apologies.

The irony of apologizing for anything and everything is that others perceive you as humble, self-effacing, and oh so nice. The feedback that emanates from this behavior is a narcotic that calms your fears that someone will be upset with you. The result? You do it even more as an insurance policy against conflict with people. The problem is that this root fear of conflict and the behavior that covers it only piles up unresolved, real issues that apologies and accommodation can't resolve between human beings. Eventually, the fuse burns quietly closer to the powder keg of emotions that covering behaviors can't cover for anymore and—*boom!*—another relationship abruptly ends for good.

When you notice yourself being overly accommodating or banking apologies to insulate yourself from potential conflict(s), you can preempt this hack of your spiritual and emotional system by stepping back and asking yourself some questions:

- Where is this coming from?
- What belief is driving this behavior?
- Where does that thinking come from?
- How do my relationship with God and his love for me address that fear?

Put pen to paper as you think this through so you can have a more tangible experience. This writing exercise accomplishes two things: (1) it records your reflections visually, and (2) it provides a guideline for next steps. Lastly, talk to God about your answers!

Maybe you hate conflict, but you hit back hard when you're hurt . . . and then you always end up having to apologize. You don't talk about it, but your feelings are hurt a lot. You're like a living bruise that gets bumped into, and God help the unfortunate soul who unwittingly said or did the wrong thing at the wrong time. You don't want to be a complainer. But under the surface, you feel disrespected. You feel left out of discussions. You feel that people are insensitive. You feel you don't catch any breaks. You feel like you're kept out of the loop. Others don't realize how hard you work or the burdens you bear. You feel underappreciated. You feel you take care of everyone else, but no one takes care of you. You feel like people don't understand you. You don't feel visible enough.

All these feelings you walk around with are like a barrel drum of highly flammable liquid nitrogen that just needs a little friction and a spark to ignite. All that is required is a human agent to make contact. Once the spark is ignited, you say awful things you regret and then wonder where those words came from and why you didn't have the capacity to hold back. You do things that feel and look like a textbook overreaction to others. You kill a fly with a rocket launcher. Then an old friend called regret shows up at the porch of your mind, rings the doorbell, and invites himself in.

When you've let resentment fester too long and you find yourself unleashing disproportionate anger on someone, you can repair the breach by following the tried-and-true advice of Scripture: Own it and apologize. The Bible calls it "swear[ing] to [your] own hurt" or sacrificing ego for reconciliation and relationship.[4] Just do it! Then after you own the fracture and pursue repair, ask for help from someone. Go have coffee with a friend and explain what happened and how you reacted. Sometimes God uses a simple conversation with a trusted friend or counselor to draw the root of the reaction upward to the surface. Dealing with the root is always preferable to experiencing the symptom again.

You Try to Impress People by Creating a Persona but Are a Nervous Wreck

Most insecure people don't "present" as insecure. You have a schtick or special way of behaving that suggests you know who you are, you are happy with who you are, you are competent and confident, and you want others to know it! You only become insecure when people really get to know you or see you in action on a regular basis. How do I know this insecurity so well? Because that was me! I was the life of the party. I was a three-sport varsity athlete. I was social. I was intelligent. I had money in the bank that I earned. I was also deeply terrified that no one would accept me, so I became the person who did things—unhealthy things—that would ensure the acceptance of others. Then I became a believer in Jesus. I wish I could say that all of those pathologies went away, but they didn't. I just adopted a new set of behaviors that would get me accepted and admired in this new ecosystem of faith. Being associated with all things Jesus was a huge help. He had visibility and credibility to pad my insecurity. I recognized what people did to gain approval and acceptance as believers, and I quickly set about mastering them. Bible knowledge. Bible studies (attending and leading them). Evangelism. Leadership positions. Risky missions trips. Full-time ministry. Teaching. Seminary.

All healthy things.

Don't get me wrong. I was a Christian who believed in the person and work of Christ, the power of the gospel, and the mission of reaching the lost. The problem was that my motives were mixed—a sure sign of insecurity. The why behind what I was doing was questionable. I know God questioned my motives, because so many times I felt like an impostor, but I could never admit the worst about myself. That would implode the image, and then what would happen to the schtick? Like all other insecurities and fears, the schtick ended up taking over. When that happened, I had to end my schtick and start having the conversation we're having right now. Rough. But God never gave up on the impostor; he saw the energy and need in me that his love could work with!

God sees past your behavior to the real you and the real reason you do what you do. When it comes to self-confrontation, just remember that calling out your own mixed motives is a spiritually healthy thing to do. If a hidden camera followed me around all day, you would no doubt hear me talking to myself and saying things like "Sure, Kenny" or "Are you going to lie to yourself?" I assure you that I don't have a dissociative disorder or multiple personalities, but I do have mixed motives, and they must be confronted. Equally effective is understanding that God not only sees the reasons and motives for my actions but will hold me accountable for them. In fact, the Bible says he will disclose the motives behind what I did on earth. Whoa! God only wants each of us to be the person he created us to be. That's the journey. God's love throws open the door to discovering that person. Walk through it!

You Define Yourself by What Other People Think of You

This is another red flag that you can easily dismiss because everybody cares, at some level, about the opinions of others. You may be a man of faith and a follower of Jesus, but functionally you're a disciple of other people's opinions about you. That's the true controlling factor in your life. You want to be perceived positively, and you adjust your behavior to match what you believe other people want. It's not about substance, convictions, or real beliefs you share; it's about *perception*. Based on your behaviors, people believe you are "with" them, and it pleases you that they are pleased with you. You may have heard the term *codependent* or the personality type called a *pleaser*. Both mean the same thing. You're unsure of yourself, so you defer to other people and let them define you or tell you who you are at the expense of who God says you are. Their opinion or approval comes before his. You want everyone to like and accept you, but that's an unrealistic and dysfunctional pursuit, because every human being is good and bad. Some people will like you, and some won't.

On the flip side, if people don't respond positively enough to you, you may read into it and assume they have a low estimation of you. That's called taking things personally. You think a lot about what you think people think of you. Like the other insecurities and fears mentioned before, living in fear of what others think of you means they determine how you perceive yourself—not God and his love. When that happens, you let what others say about you be the truth, and you remain insecure and feel lost. Your identity has been hijacked.

Evil forces will seek out, probe, and exploit every unhealed wound or insecurity we have. These forces traffic in fear. That is why it's mission critical to recognize the patterns in our behaviors that tell us some "thing" is taking over. One, some, or all of these patterns may apply to you. But recognition is not enough.

You need to authenticate who you truly are on a day-by-day, moment-by-moment basis. Every man's security in God's love will be attacked, but not every man knows how to build a spiritual firewall that prevents rogue fears from getting into his mind and heart and taking root.

Each day is a new battle, and it's waged between your ears.

Let the morning bring me word of your unfailing love,
    for I have put my trust in you.
Show me the way I should go,
    for to you I entrust my life.[5]

Boot Up Each Day and Authenticate Your Identity

Strong love between you and God requires the mind.

Jesus replied: "'Love the Lord your God with all your heart and with all your soul and with all your mind.'"[6]

Mary said:
"My soul glorifies the Lord
    and my spirit rejoices in God my Savior,
for he has been mindful
    of the humble state of his servant."[7]

The Israelites did evil in the eyes of the LORD; they forgot the LORD their God and served the Baals and the Asherahs.[8]

God is always mindful of us, crazy about us, and thinking about us. It's mind-boggling how quickly that truest truth gets lost in the white noise of our existence. As men, we must intentionally

rget about God and his love. Each day is a war
ng or forgetting. When God's people actively and
emember him and his love for them, and thank him
ses its moorings in our spirits. When we forget him,
our minds are infiltrated by lies, the lies are believed, and the new
(Godless) beliefs are reflected in behaviors that harm our relationships with God and with one another.

Each day we "boot up" our lives. Our eyes open. Our minds
turn on. We start thinking. We elect or "click on" thoughts we
want to act on. Then we start doing what we're thinking. Where
we take our minds each day as we start to think is a vital aspect of
remaining in God's love and acceptance. We can start each day by
intentionally remembering God, calling to mind his love, dwelling on what he has done, marveling over our relationship with
him, and *authenticating* that he fully accepts, fully loves, and fully
defines us. Or we can start the day *not* remembering. The "not"
part should sober us and move us to action.

Here's why:

> You will keep in perfect peace
>   all who trust in you,
>   all whose thoughts are fixed on you.[9]

The opposite of living in peace is living in fear and anxiety.
God says perfect peace can be yours if you boot up your mind and
authenticate his presence in your life by directing your thoughts
toward him. This is how your inner man and the truest truths
about you must be locked down. Conversely, the threats to your
inner emotional security must be thwarted and defeated. Each
day you wake up and boot up your mind, heart, and soul, a spiritual discipline of double authentication of your identity must
happen immediately and on a moment-by-moment basis using

Spirit-empowered weapons and actions. These actions, just like my regular authentications for access to my computer, *must* be taken to protect your core person, core beliefs, and core understandings of who you are in God's love.

Forces in the spiritual, natural, and cultural realms *will repeatedly attempt* to take advantage of any vulnerability, fear, or insecurity to break in and hijack your inner man. The result? That force will assume control for dark purposes. The target? The highest-value truths about how God feels about you, what he has done for you, and what he intends for you are at the top of the list. Evil seeks to neutralize these thoughts in you. For believers, it means there is an everyday attack on your view of self and God.

Big evil loves to mute big truth. Remembering God's love and acceptance each day locks it out.

Remembering Is a Daily Joy

Boot up every day by declaring the truest truth as an authentication of God's presence and love.

This is the day which the LORD has made;
let's rejoice and be glad in it.[10]

Yet this I call to mind
    and therefore I have hope:
Because of the LORD's great love we are not consumed,
    for his compassions never fail.
They are new every morning;
    great is your faithfulness.[11]

Every day has morning, and every morning God's love is waiting to greet you. Starting your daily thinking process by remembering God and his love is to love him with your mind, demonstrate that you care about him, and run the hacker into a wall he cannot penetrate. Not today, Satan. Not today, liar. Not today, fear.

Remembering Is a Daily Battle

Earth is war. C. S. Lewis put it succinctly this way: "Enemy-occupied territory—that is what this world is. Christianity is the story of how the rightful king has landed, you might say landed in disguise, and is calling us all to take part in a great campaign of sabotage."[12] After you boot up your mind and speak out the truest truth about God's presence and love (literally), it's time to guard and defend your mind against the hacker, who wants to plant thoughts and make suggestions that will compromise who you are in God's love.

> The world is unprincipled. It's dog-eat-dog out there! The world doesn't fight fair. But we don't live or fight our battles that way—never have and never will. The tools of our trade aren't for marketing or manipulation, but they are for demolishing that entire massively corrupt culture. We use our powerful God-tools for smashing warped philosophies, tearing down barriers erected against the truth of God, fitting every loose thought and emotion and impulse into the structure of life shaped by Christ. Our tools are ready at hand for clearing the ground of every obstruction and building lives of obedience into maturity.[13]

> The mouth of the righteous utters wisdom,
>   And his tongue speaks justice.
> The law of his God is in his heart;
>   His steps do not slip.[14]

When a thought comes into your mind that attacks the reality of your relationship with God, his presence, his love, his plan, or his ability to work out all things for your good, declare this with your mouth openly, energetically, and with faith in the truth. Jesus did this when the master hacker tried to break into his mind. He unloaded what the hacker knew was true. You can do the same— word for word.

> Jesus said . . . , "Go away, Satan! For it is written: 'You shall worship the Lord your God and serve Him only.'"[15]

Remembering Is Discipline and Lifestyle

When I wake up every day, I want the hacker to say to himself, *Oh, crap! He's up!* If you had a hidden camera in my house and were to follow my wake-up routine, within roughly the first thirty seconds, you would hear me say these words: "This is the day the Lord has made. [I] will rejoice and be glad in it."[16] You might hear this another two or three times, mixed in with other choice morning sounds, like my espresso maker, my electric toothbrush, and a flushing sound. It is not a ritual. It's me battling for my identity and setting my mind. It is a must. It's a daily thing. And if you aren't starting your day letting the hacker know who you are and that you recognize him, I respectfully challenge you to adopt my routine declaration every morning or find a truth of your own to stick in his face. Sound visceral? The hacker doesn't play nickel poker. He is out to steal your thinking about God and hopes you don't remember to get your day started with his truth.

If "It is written . . ." was useful for Jesus in shutting down a satanic assault on his mind, what Jesus modeled for us is meant for us. If we want to fight for our connection to God like Jesus, we need to act like Jesus.

So if you're serious about living this new resurrection life with Christ, *act* like it. Pursue the things over which Christ presides. Don't shuffle along, eyes to the ground, absorbed with the things right in front of you. Look up, and be alert to what is going on around Christ—that's where the action is. See things from *his* perspective.[17]

As water reflects your face,
    so your mind shows what kind of person you are.[18]

Be determined not to let the ultimate spiritual hacker mess with the operating system of God's love inside you. Jesus didn't let the hacker mess with him, and neither should you. You are what you think. You do what you think. Speak to the fears and lies attacking God's presence and love as often and as aggressively as you need to.

A Firewall Declaration

I am in Christ. The blood of Jesus was shed for me. It covers me and seals me. I am a son of the Most High God. I am fully accepted by God. I am fully loved by God. I am fully defined by God. It is written, "Love the Lord your God with all your heart, all your soul, all your mind, and all your strength."[19] That is who I am, and that is what I will do today and every day. To Jesus be all the glory.

6

THE HEAD AND THE HEART

The Inner Chasm

KNOWING IS DIFFERENT FROM KNOWLEDGE.

I know a lot *about* snowboarding. Imagine yourself asking me, "Do you think I should try snowboarding?" I could say, "I think snowboarding is great" and then proceed to explain the origins of snowboarding. The history. The physics. The technique. The modern snowboard versus its predecessors. The places where you can snowboard. The dangers of snowboarding. The difference between fresh powder and groomed snow. The proper ways of getting on and off a chairlift. The difference between goofy and regular stances on a snowboard. Stopping. Carving. S-turning. Clicking out of your bindings. And on and on ad nauseam.

That would be a rough conversation for you. Why?

Because my knowledge is limited to facts, education, reason, objects, and memory. It's about the head. It's about being able to explain things objectively. Why make this distinction? Knowledge based on information alone provides partial familiarity; there is an emotional distance and incompleteness when you only know facts and details *about* something. In fact, I would sincerely hope that you would respectfully pause our hypothetical convo after a few minutes and ask me, "So, Kenny, have you ever actually physically snowboarded yourself?"

Knowing based on experience is a *qualitative* way to measure anything and is way better. More specifically, I would be able to tell you how awesome and wonderful snowboarding *actually* is (because I *do* snowboard) versus just describing it.

There's a big gap between "I snowboard" and "I know a lot about snowboarding."

It's a shame that when it comes to the awesome nature and power of God's love, so many Christian men (and women, for that matter) speak from their heads and not from their experience or their hearts. There's a big gap between "I actually *know* Jesus and his love" from experience and "I know a lot *about* Jesus and his love" in my brain. It's a problem, and it's tragic, especially when you understand just how much there is to experience and be strengthened by when the reality and power of God's love travel from your head to your heart on a regular basis. This journey south, whereby God's love takes the elevator in your spirit to where it can heal you and set you free emotionally and psychologically is an event the evil one fears. Why? Because both control and freedom are at stake. The devil also knows the head and heart *disconnect* makes your relationship with God one-dimensional, distant, and incomplete, and he wants to keep it that way. That is why the spiritual journey from knowledge to knowing must happen. To be secure, you must have an anchor, and that anchor isn't knowledge *about* how God fully loves, accepts, and defines you; it's about actually *knowing*—experiencing and comprehending at a heart level—the multidimensional nature of God's love inside you. What's at stake? Freedom from other influences that control your life. There is also another reason.

The head and heart *connection* is the birthright of every child of God.

News Flash: Heart Defeats Head!

Shocking victories are remembered.

Think about Muhammad Ali defeating the overwhelmingly favored Sonny Liston for the 1964 heavyweight boxing title, and the rest is, well, history. Think about the "Miracle on Ice" in 1980, when the United States defeated the former Soviet Union in Olympic ice hockey. Fast-forward to the 2007 Fiesta Bowl upset of the Oklahoma Sooners by Boise State. (No college sports fan who saw it will ever forget it.) In the UFC world, think about Holly Holm's stunning victory over previously unbeaten Ronda Rousey—not only the biggest upset in UFC history, but one of the biggest in sports history. For theater people: Who in their right minds would think an off-Broadway production that draws heavily from hip-hop and casts nonwhite actors as America's founding fathers would become the phenomenon known as *Hamilton*. Think about Donald Trump defeating overwhelming favorite and presidential shoe-in Hillary Clinton in the 2016 US presidential election—few saw that coming, including me. You get the picture.

Pure shock and awe. Why? Because people made assumptions.

Whether or not we admit it, we all make assumptions about whether certain things about us or around us will change. We "handicap" our chances. We let the limiting voices versus the optimistic voices sway our thinking. We let the clouds make us forget there is sunshine behind them. We let the past permanently shape our thinking about the future. This human habit of making and acting on assumptions leaks into and impacts our spiritual lives.

Some of us can't envision any other experience with God than what we already know or have known. So our unlimited God becomes a closed system. Or perhaps we've seen God move mightily in one area of our lives, but somehow his desire or power is restricted in other areas. So we stop praying and trusting for breakthroughs. The saddest thing about this is that as men of faith, we believe that powerful shifts or victories in our identity, circumstances, health, events, fortunes, emotions, or spiritual lives can happen, but deep down is an undercurrent of very real pessimism, ambivalence, fear, or doubt that is operating but is unexpressed and unidentified.

In our minds, we have made assumptions about God and how he wants to work. Our lives in God begin to reflect our assumptions about God—wrong ones. The result? Our heads and assumptions defeat our hearts and potential new experiences.

It's called going through the motions, and Jesus takes it personally: "These people honor me with their lips, but their hearts are far from me."[1]

Fortunately, our assumptions about God don't limit him in any way, but they do limit us when it comes to winning the battle to become secure, mature, and complete in his love. In fact, God wants his love to produce monumental upsets and conquer the things that are defeating our fullest experience of him. He wants our living in his acceptance to blow open the spiritual floodgates. Think of God's love as the knockout punch that sends the big fears in your life falling to the canvas, incapacitated and unable to rise. If you're a football fan, imagine God's love as the key block that springs your life into regular breakaway touchdowns versus tackles for loss.

Think of your life being an upset victory.

It's the you nobody saw coming, including yourself. The only thing stopping a strong and visible shift in you through a strong identity and security in God's love is your assumptions about what he wants to do and what his love has already accomplished. You just can't get out of your own head long enough for your heart to see and receive what he wants to give you. As you read this, you might sense a tension welling up inside you. If so, just know that it isn't something to fear, because on the other side of that feeling is a new or renewed life God wants for you. That's why the tension is there! What you're feeling is God's desire for you. What desire is that? His desire for great wins and upsets. But let's be even more specific. *He wants your heart to defeat your head through his love.*

In a shocking fashion and in ways specific only to you, God has set the stage for the spiritual upset victory that—in your history—will stun the naysayers, the critics, the doubters, the haters, the analysts, the people betting against you, the people (including you) who expect your life to take a predicted trajectory, and the devil himself. Why does God want this spiritual disruption to happen so badly? Because he knows that head knowledge of his love without a deep and pervasive encounter with his love in your heart renders it useless. *That* is the shock-and-awe encounter God wants for all of us.

God told them, "I've never quit loving you and never will. Expect love, love, and more love!"[2]

How do I pull off this massive upset of my heart over my head? Answer: A pouring. A grasping. A knowing. A filling. A sensing.

Hope does not put us to shame, because God's love has been poured out into our hearts through the Holy Spirit, who has been given to us.[3]

I pray that you, being rooted and established in love, may have power, together with all the Lord's holy people, to grasp how wide and long and high and deep is the love of Christ, and to know this love that surpasses knowledge— that you may be filled to the measure of all the fullness of God.[4]

Though you have not seen him, you love him; and even though you do not see him now, you believe in him and are filled with an inexpressible and glorious joy.[5]

Hope—the sustaining kind we feel in a deep place—comes from the love of God being *poured* into us through faith in Jesus. If your faith in Jesus is present, the foundation for your victory has already been worked into your heart through God's Spirit, and it simply needs to be worked out. That's the biggest *if* of all. The Spirit of Christ must be *present in you* for the process to *work out through you*. If you can say, "I'm hopeful," because of God's presence in your life right now, that is a great sign of faith and moves the ball well downfield. You are in possession of faith—the all-important "ball" without which you cannot score.

The gap between our heads and our hearts—the possession of faith versus the real power in our lives—is seen most clearly in the midst of suffering and challenges. Think 2020. In what was globally and personally the most disruptive year in the modern era, the possession of faith and the functional power of faith were placed in a crunch-time scenario, catching most believers by surprise. In a Joshua Fund survey taken during the COVID-19 pandemic, a substantial number of people indicated that the crisis was their wake-up call to renew their faith and begin taking action spiritually.[6] When the unplanned happens, when the unwelcome lands on our doorstep, when unfathomable loss shatters our world— these are the times when our inability to control events around us creates vulnerability, and that vulnerability creates an openness to the things God wants to accomplish in us. One of those things, without a doubt, is that we get reacquainted with his deep concern and love for us, which is available now.

That energy to seize all that our faith in Christ has secured is what is meant by seeking to *grasp* or comprehend all dimensions of God's powerful love within us. We have it, but we just can't seem to access it personally. This is one of the more frustrating failures in faith—knowing what we have, hearing about what we possess in Christ, seeing other people thrive and change, but lacking in experience what we know and see happening in others. In my experience, the two words that best describe how that feels are *depressing* and *isolating*. When we lack a promised experience from God, it makes us question the validity of Christ's power and presence in our lives. It also makes us vulnerable to all forms of spiritual attack by the evil one, who senses our seeming helplessness. But we are not helpless in reality.

We just have to ask.

Jesus answered [the woman at the well], "If you knew the gift of God and who it is that asks you for a drink, you would have asked him and he would have given you living water."

"Sir," the woman said, "you have nothing to draw with and the well is deep. Where can you get this living water?"[7]

On the last and greatest day of the festival, Jesus stood and said in a loud voice, "Let anyone who is thirsty come to me and drink. Whoever believes in me, as Scripture has said, rivers of living water will flow from within them."[8]

Jesus wants us to take the spiritual initiative. Paul, the greatest spiritual coach to ever live, was painfully desperate for the believers he knew to grasp God's love—or, in a twist on that desire, to not fail to grasp the enormity of this head-to-heart connection. He wanted for them what he himself had experienced: a breaking through into every dimension of God's love. He saw what they were missing and was sounding an alarm. Jesus' love has dimensions that need to be experienced—width, length, height, and depth.

Do you know the dimensions of God's love?

Width of love means that God's love has the ability to cover things. It covers our shame, guilt, and despair over sin. It covers every adversity and cross we must bear, as well as every success we savor. It covers our flaws of character. It covers the past and redeems it. It covers the future and reserves it for us in Christ. It spreads out across the entire breadth of our lives, just as east and west perpetually extend and never come to an end. How wide is God's love? "For God so loved the world."[9] *Limitless* and *infinite* mean that God has enough width in his love to *permanently* cover every part of us that gives rise to fear. We need this covering. Does your heart want to know the width of his love now and forever?

Length of love means that no matter when you believed and received your deposit of God's love, it will continue as long as you exist. Wherever you travel, however long you are on earth, and for the duration of eternity, it's there. You can't outrun it. No sin can exceed its length. Satan wants you to think that God's love is like a tape measure that hits a stopping point when you fail to measure up to God's standards, or your own. If you are using the measuring tape of your own standards, the world's standards, or the standards others place on you, it will definitely run out of length. But there is only one standard God accepts: Christ's. We need this lengthy, infinitely extending standard of love that outmeasures the silly standards we place on ourselves. Does your heart want to *know* the length of God's love right now?

Height of love means that the fear, self-doubt, insecurity, or just plain ignorance that pull us down have been broken, and we are free to ascend to new heights in Christ and in our lives. Remember our earlier conversation about how God's love has seated us with Christ, and we have the best seat in the house? Love did that. The height of God's love that has elevated us to this position has given us access and authority before God himself. What love! What a place to be able to enter through faith. What confidence we have from *that place* to tackle the worst days, the worst memories, the worst feelings, and the worst parts of ourselves. What a place to have the big picture. To have the perspective of God. To be able to sit with him outside of time and space and see what he sees. Like a father who carries his child on his shoulders, God lifts us up and rests us on his shoulders so that we can see clearly through his love what we couldn't see when we existed at the ground level of head knowledge. It's a different view from the height of his love—a better, more refreshing, and more thrilling position. We all need to feel the lifting, the new air at elevation, the thrill of seeing things from God's perspective through his love. Does your heart want to *know* that lift and height right now?

Depth of love means that Jesus left his high position in heaven to descend into the mess of earth—my mess and your mess. Shoulder to shoulder, pain to pain, loss to loss, and weakness to weakness. He knows the depths of every emotion connected to the spectrum of our experience as human beings. That makes him a perfect friend *and* Savior. That's deep! He understands us at both levels—from the captain's deck on top of the world to the engine room shoveling coal. The Servant-King left high to go low so he could know us, be with us in the mess, and suffer with us and for us. Without his courage and his deep love for us, we would doubt that he cares about our suffering from a place of nonsuffering and perfection. But that was never the plan. He came to earth to feel our feelings, to see what we see, to know the good, despise the bad, and be the target of the vicious. Every injustice we have felt, he felt and feels. He knows every joy and victory as well. Every temptation, too. With no exceptions, he has felt everything we feel; if not, he couldn't understand us. We need this deep and pervasive love that belongs to Jesus alone, and that he delivers to us through his Spirit alone. Is your heart ready for a deep connection with someone whose love extends far beyond all you supposedly know about him to what he fully knows and understands about you?

Wide. Long. High. Deep.

Knowing this love in our hearts surpasses head knowledge. God wants our heart knowledge of his love to be active in the fullest possible way and rise to the fullest measure to engulf every aspect of our cognitive, subjective, psychological, and emotional selves to the fullest measure in the fullest possible way. Does that feel overwhelming? Maybe for us, but not for God, because he has already placed the massive aquifer of his love underneath our lives in Christ. He wants to remind us that his love is available for us to tap into. If we feel we've been sold short, it wasn't God's choice but ours. He has done his part. We don't have to understand why God loves us in such a lavish way, but we do need to remove the obstacles so we can experience the healing, securing, and freeing effects of his love.

> "Build up, build up, prepare the road!
> Remove the obstacles out of the way of my people."[10]

Strongholds and Strangleholds

The strongholds in our heads are strangleholds that choke out the love of God in our hearts.

The fullness of God's love is available to us, but streams of bad thinking about ourselves and God have been flowing unabated for months, years, or perhaps decades. When anything is allowed to flow so forcefully for so long, it creates an emotional rut—a habit or pattern of thinking and behaving that is dull, unproductive, and hard to change. The Bible calls embedded patterns of thinking "strongholds."[11] The strongholds in our lives manifest themselves in psychological and emotional ways. They aren't hard to spot. These mental ruts come in all shapes and sizes: doubt, rejection, irrational fears, poor self-esteem, pride, stubbornness, a victim mentality, or defeatism, to name just a few. They almost always correspond to a lie Satan has established in our thinking that we count as true. These false beliefs lead to behaviors that alienate us from God's love and people. These restrictive mental ruts limit our ability to know God in the fullest way and become complete in his love.

Note to self: God wants these strongholds gone. Eliminated. Destroyed. Vaporized.

> We use God's mighty weapons, not worldly weapons, to knock down the strongholds of human reasoning and to destroy false arguments. We destroy every proud obstacle that keeps people from knowing God. We capture their rebellious thoughts and teach them to obey Christ.[12]

That's strong language that requires some strong and practical application questions:

- Is God asking me to destroy wrong ways of thinking and false assumptions about myself?
- Does he want me to proactively eliminate all misperceptions about his ability to change me?
- Is he directing me to challenge the fears that produce so much anxiety and distance with him and others?

Yes, yes, and yes! There is no YouTube video for this. But you can still see how it's done by watching what Jesus did:

> The devil came [to Jesus] and said to him, "If you are the Son of God, tell these stones to become loaves of bread." But Jesus told him, "No! The Scriptures say,
>
> 'People do not live by bread alone,
>   but by every word that comes from the mouth of God.'"[13]

Witness the annihilation of a potential stronghold. The devil made a suggestion that would have compromised Jesus' relationship with his Father and diminished his connection to the Father's love. That suggestion appealed to the physically and emotionally fatigued Jesus, but the real goal was to destroy Jesus' relationship with his Father. In response, Jesus brought to bear the spiritual weapon of God's truth against the inferior power of Satan's lie by refusing to believe it and intentionally replacing it with God's revealed will in Scripture.

Notice Jesus' appeal to Scripture. Jesus wasn't a big user of religious words when interacting with people or talking about how the Kingdom of God works. He spoke simply and directly in everyday language, but he also recognized that certain situations demand the full force of God's Word—especially when something precious is threatened. Jesus could have given two possible responses to the suggestion.

Response A: "You're right. That's true. I need to act on what you've suggested."

Response B: "You're wrong. That's a lie, and I forcefully reject it. Let me tell you what God thinks of that suggestion of yours."

That's how you destroy a potential or existing stronghold.

There was a time in my life when mental suggestions were left unexamined and weren't passed through the filter of my relationship with God. Like letting terrorists in through a porous, undermanaged security checkpoint, my mind didn't inspect thoughts for approval or call in for questioning some long-held beliefs about myself that prevented me from living free and secure in God's love. In hindsight, I see what a horrible message my laziness and lack of diligence were sending to God. In essence, my message was "Our relationship and the love you have poured into me aren't worth seeking out, experiencing, or defending." It makes me shudder now, but God's patience with me was just as limitless, long, wide, and deep as his love.

Gently, lovingly, graciously, and tenderly, he invited me into the process we've been discussing in this chapter. He helped me see the many lies I believed about myself and how his love was uniquely able to destroy the dysfunctional thought patterns preventing me from having the heart-level experience with his love that I wanted so desperately. His love had yet to take the elevator all the way down into the deep parts of my heart and emotions. Because of fear and the embedded strongholds in my mind, I was still protecting myself. My guard was up, but my experience with God's love was down.

It was a head game, and I was losing.

How about you? Perhaps there are places in your life that you haven't let anyone, including God, into because you can't control what happens next, or you don't know what it means for you *not* to protect yourself. You've thought this way too long. It's too familiar. It's what you know. It's a stronghold. You might hear a familiar tape playing in your head that says, *Why rock the boat now? This is who you are, man.*

On the other side of the spectrum, perhaps you've known

Jesus so long that your rut is religious, not emotional. You've been keeping an infinite and loving God in your cultural-religious box, and that has limited a fresh encounter and experience with his love. You're so familiar with religious culture and practice that you're almost prideful about it. That's your barrier to experiencing God's love.

Both of these patterns are strongholds the evil one hopes you leave undisturbed, because they accomplish his goal of keeping you chained to the lies you believe. But God is waiting for you at either end of this dysfunctional spectrum. The elimination of either stronghold—sinner or saint—starts with a willingness to look in that ever-so-uncomfortable mirror and stay there.

This is your step of faith. This is your call. This is your move.

Don't fool yourself into thinking that you are a listener when you are anything but, letting the Word go in one ear and out the other. *Act* on what you hear! Those who hear and don't act are like those who glance in the mirror, walk away, and two minutes later have no idea who they are, what they look like.

But whoever catches a glimpse of the revealed counsel of God—the free life!—even out of the corner of his eye, and sticks with it, is no distracted scatterbrain but a man or woman of action. That person will find delight and affirmation in the action.[14]

It's time to break through the head-heart barrier and make the effort to become the man God created you to be:

- A courageous self-examiner who is willing to address the obvious gaps between what God says and how you live in his love

- A man who senses when things are "off" spiritually, emotionally, or relationally and promptly faces them, not fearing the outcome in light of the permanence of God's acceptance
- An authentic believer who doesn't feel the need to fake it in different dimensions of your life or say things are "awesome" or "great" for fear of what others will think
- A man who is able to let down your defenses with God and people for the sake of spiritual growth, accountability, and transformation

This is what God's love calls us to.

So we know and rely on the love God has for us.
God is love. Whoever lives in love lives in God, and God in them. This is how love is made complete among us so that we will have confidence on the day of judgment: In this world we are like Jesus.[15]

The victory of heart over head feels, well, new. It feels like Jesus. This newness has three dimensions:

1. *A new knowing of God's love.* Successful head-to-heart victories involve connecting to God's love in a new way. The big difference is that you're aware of it personally rather than remotely or to impress others. You sense it personally instead of speculating about it personally or guessing and wondering about it personally. Those days are over. You are now persuaded and convinced that God loves you completely. You know it through firsthand experience versus knowing *about* it. You know it because you believe in it and act on your belief. The process of salvation through God's love *worked into* you by faith is now being *worked out* in you by faith. Your relationship with God started with believing in his love.

You trusted that his love, in its incredible width, length, height, and depth, was for you and saved you. Now you believe that same love and acceptance will continue to sustain you, heal you, and free you from dysfunctional thinking, reframe your character, and make you more like Christ. Jesus knows it when he sees it in your life and declares what he sees. This is what you know:

> "The Father himself loves you because you have loved
> me [Jesus] and have believed that I came from God."[16]

2. *A new relying on God's love.* Knowing God's love by experience leads to a newer, more confident reliance on that love at all times and in all situations. With fear-filled strongholds destroyed, you find yourself trusting God in spite of the past, in the face of present challenges, and in spite of some negative feelings connected to life here on earth. His love is a fortress, a refuge, and a stronghold in your life. You believe that his love is not circumstantial. Adversity or prosperity don't affect how he feels about you, and because that is true, he is working things out in your best interests. You are in the center of his love, and you're wise to remain there. The alternative would be to remain in your head! You are steadied by his love. Your obedience is sturdy, not flaky. Your joy is full versus fleeting. This is what you rely on:

> "As the Father has loved me, so have I [Jesus] loved you.
> Now remain in my love. If you keep my commands, you
> will remain in my love, just as I have kept my Father's
> commands and remain in his love. I have told you this
> so that my joy may be in you and that your joy may be
> complete."[17]

THE HEAD AND THE HEART

3. *A new living in God's love.* Completely living in God's love looks different from the way you once lived. Your heart is convinced when your head doubts, and you make more decisions out of faith than fear. You live less divided between what you believe and how you think and behave. You're no longer worried about what others think. You more easily break the pattern of immature masculinity and experience greater freedom because your actions show loyalty to Jesus and love for people. You have stopped living to please people and are striving instead to please your heavenly Father, as Jesus modeled for you. You're freely and confidently out-living and outloving a self-absorbed world. What is most precious and valuable to you is your connection with God and working out that connection with others. Love is flowing in your heart and is fully in charge. This is what you're living in:

"A new command I [Jesus] give you: Love one another. As I have loved you, so you must love one another. By this everyone will know that you are my disciples, if you love one another."[18]

Let no debt remain outstanding, except the continuing debt to love one another, for whoever loves others has fulfilled the law. The commandments, "You shall not commit adultery," "You shall not murder," "You shall not steal," "You shall not covet," and whatever other command there may be, are summed up in this one command: "Love your neighbor as yourself."[19]

Knowing God's love firsthand through experience, relying on it, and living in it by faith have given your heart the improbable and stunning victory over your head. Your overwhelmingly favored opponent has fallen. People are stunned. Doubters are silenced. Skeptics stay quiet. Even your own doubts are muted. Fear has lost. God's love has permanently prevailed.

Do you believe in miracles?

You are one.

Heavenly Father,

I want to experience a new connection to your love. For reasons that you alone know, I have strongholds in my mind that prevent your love from reaching broken, parched, and wounded places within. Through your Son, Jesus, I ask that all obstacles between what I know in my head and what I experience in my heart be removed. I want the fullest force of your love to flood my spirit. Remove the ruts in my mind. Do what you must so that I can sense the promise of your Word and Spirit. Move in my life in a new way. By the power of your Spirit, testify to my inner man that I am yours and you are mine. I want to live boldly and confidently before you and before people. Here I am—flood my mind. Go to the fear. Go to the wounds. Go to the losses. Release all of your love in every part of me, so I can live fully in it. Thank you for hearing my prayer and answering me through your Spirit. Here I am. Fill me. Amen.

ACTING SECURE

7

EACH DAY

The Secure Root and Grow

"WHY DID MY TREE JUST DIE?"

That was my Google search and reflects an area of disappointment in my life. Let's just say, if trees and plants could talk as they leave the nursery, they would declare to their fellow trees and plants on my big roller cart, "Nice knowing you."

That scenario speaks to life expectancy. My wife and I are notorious for sending plants and trees we purchase to their demise, because the sad fact is that we are lazy gardeners and bad green thumbs. Our visions are great and our intentions are good, but the reality is that plants, flowers, and trees just don't last under our care. Only the most hardy—like the shrubbery that doesn't bloom—will survive. Trust me when I say we've made major attempts to beautify and landscape, but after the initial wave of planting, most of our newly installed friends lose their sizzle and shine and end up in the "green waste" recycle bin.

I almost gave up on planting new flowers, trees, or bushes in my front and back yards because I didn't want to disappoint myself *again*. Planted things have one of two destinies. They will either end up pleasing the person who planted them or causing frustration and disappointment. Every gardener wants each living thing that has been planted to realize the vision and promise connected to its special selection.

> Make a tree good and its fruit will be good, or make a tree bad and its fruit will be bad, for a tree is recognized by its fruit. . . . A good man brings good things out of the good stored up in him, and an evil man brings evil things out of the evil stored up in him.[1]

> The nation of Israel is the vineyard of the LORD of Heaven's Armies.
>   The people of Judah are his pleasant garden.
> He expected a crop of justice,
>   but instead he found oppression.
> He expected to find righteousness,
>   but instead he heard cries of violence.[2]

> [Jesus said,] "I am the true vine, and my Father is the gardener. He cuts off every branch in me that bears no fruit, while every branch that does bear fruit he prunes so that it will be even more fruitful. . . .
>   "If you do not remain in me, you are like a branch that is thrown away and withers; such branches are picked up, thrown into the fire and burned."[3]

The Gardener is God, and we are the plants. We are planted in Christ. He has a vision and hope for you.

Will we please him or frustrate him?

The Planted Ones

Mango and orange.

I can see out my dining-room window the new orange and mango trees I recently planted. They've joined the lemon and avocado trees I worked into the front and back yards. Mango serves me well because I'm a Pacific Islander and grew up opening large crates of large mangoes shipped from the islands. The orange connection has roots in my past as well. I grew up with a huge orange tree in my backyard that we ate from all the time. If you have a good orange, you know it can be consumed as is, sliced and put in beer, squeezed for juice, or zested for recipes. My newly planted trees have meaning and value to me, which is why I specifically picked them for my yard. As far as size goes, my new trees are "tweeners"—not baby trees, but not adults, which means they're bigger, and we can see results sooner.

Will this time be different?

These trees could be the ones that reach their fullest potential and will be around for my future grandkids to enjoy and eat the fruit. Because of my track record and personal connection with trees, as well as my fruit-filled dreams about them, I planted them with a lot of hope. I *never* thought I would feel this way about two fledgling fruit trees. I'm also thinking about the unique process taking place below the ground, which I'm trusting to go well so that what happens above the ground will produce what I'm hoping for.

Sometimes I wonder if God is teaching me a thing or two about gardening. It's as if we are the garden of his delight—his gardening trophies. He plants us in his private yard, has a special connection to us, has selected us for his purposes, and is filled with hope as we mysteriously experience his supernatural growth process.

> Just as you accepted Christ Jesus as your Lord, you must continue to follow him. Let your roots grow down into him, and let your lives be built on him. Then your faith will grow strong in the truth you were taught, and you will overflow with thankfulness.[4]

Accepting. Continuing. Rooting. Building. Growing. Overflowing.

This is the process God has started in our lives and is pursuing with each one of us. He is a self-described Gardener with a clear vision and an equally clear hope for his planted ones. It's personal, too. He selected you at the same time you were selecting him—mysteriously cool. He chose you to be in Christ at the same time you were choosing to be in Christ—providence. He planted the fullness of his love in you—the fullest expression loaded into the seeds of your salvation—and is committed to seeing his love fully worked out in your life. All him. He sees a dynamic process happening right now in you, as you search in his Word for the nutrients and living water you need. He sees you taking the life-giving truth of his love into your root system and watches as it works its way to the surface. The Gardener knows his planted ones, and the planted ones experience the care and loving commitment of the Gardener overseeing the process.

The vision is being realized.

> There has never been the slightest doubt in my mind that the God who started this great work in you would keep at it and bring it to a flourishing finish on the very day Christ Jesus appears.[5]

The God who began this work in you has the end in mind.

After we accept the person and work of Christ for salvation, the upward process of transformation begins and doesn't stop until our hearts stop beating. That's why we focused earlier on the heart versus the head. Information is *not* transformation. God isn't looking primarily at what we know about him; he's looking at the love he has planted in us and where it takes us. As we are learning and growing, hidden issues and emotional processes below the "dirt" or surface of our lives can directly impact the levels of emotional growth and fruitfulness above the surface for all to see. After we take that first step of accepting the love of God in the person of Christ, the battle is to remain in his love so we can remain in God's process and fulfill his vision and hope for us. This is God's call to continue following him, which involves daily processes that cycle and recycle in our lives throughout the entire course of our earthly experience in Christ.

The Gardener's process requires a lifestyle of remaining in God's love. This lifestyle is an each-day thing that brings about fruit that reflects the source. My mango trees make mangoes. My orange tree makes oranges. Fruit reflects the source. Our fruit (our character and conduct) reflects our strongest source that feeds our root system. I trust you know at this point that our strongest source for identity, security, and maturity is the love and acceptance of God. So let's start there and see what a lifestyle of remaining in God's love looks like.

Be Rooted in Him Each Day

If you've ever seen a below-the-ground and above-the-ground rendering of a tree, it looks normal to your eye above the surface and like an X-ray below the surface. We aren't used to seeing the true reality of a strong and healthy tree—its root system. After a seed is planted in the ground, a healthy tree will show little visible growth above ground in its first years as the primary and most important root—the taproot—extends downward out of the seed. It's counterintuitive to you and me, but a tree actually has to grow *downward* before it can successfully grow *upward*. Rooting determines life and death for a tree, because if it isn't rooting well, it isn't searching for nutrients or establishing the structural foundation to support the future growth that is destined to occur above the surface.

God's process for us involves constantly rooting ourselves in his love.

As the planted ones, we are constantly searching, stretching, and extending ourselves deeper and deeper to get to the supply of God's love. Without that ongoing quest and without repeated encounters with God's love, we simply cannot grow or build the wide-ranging network of roots that sustain a strong life in Christ. Receiving Christ must be followed by a continuous process of being rooted and rerooted in his love as long as we live. So many times in my journey, I have focused on the above-ground life at the expense of the below-ground process and found myself confused as to why I seemingly didn't have breakthroughs in my character, my attitudes, and my relationships. The problem was not up top—in my head, my behaviors, my knowledge, or my disciplines. The problem was that I was missing God's love feeding deep into my heart, my emotions, and my thinking.

Being rooted in God's love is first because it is what secures his vision and hope in our hearts.

Every word, every picture, every Scripture, every principle, and every practice shared up to this point in our conversation about God's love has been for the express purpose of—you guessed it—rooting! Without a clear, personal connection to the truest truths concerning how God fully accepts, fully loves, and fully defines us through Christ, all bets are off for any lasting, healthy expression of faith in him. So many times in my life, I have had God's process upside down in my spiritual journey. A lot of building up, growing in knowledge, and overflowing in activity, and concurrently, a lot of neglecting the root system. I got top-heavy. I got focused on the outer man. I put a lot of energy into maintaining disciplines, scheduling activities, and controlling appearances. I was deep into my perceptions of what I thought the Christian life was at the expense of the Gardener's process.

This upside-down way of living fits our culture but doesn't align with God's process. The quick gains, spiritual sprints, and shiny achievements run out of gas and lose their luster in the face of mighty storms and wildfires that expose how shallow our rooting in God's love actually is. We have what we think is a life that will support us for the duration, but we're mistaken. Our shallow-rooted lives do the job—sometimes for decades—but the root system isn't able to support the persona we have so proudly built above ground. We are top-heavy. But that's just one side of the problem.

Below the ground is erosion. When we aren't rooting deeply in God's love, our unhealed fears and insecurities will take over below the surface. This creates perfect conditions for collapse and a scarcity of the Spirit. The mounting pressures of life, along with poor rooting, cause hairline fractures in the base of our spiritual lives. We can sense it happening, but with so much going on above ground, we tell ourselves, *It can't be! Look at what I've become. Look at how much I know. Look at the life I've built. I'm so disciplined. People and circumstances around me need to change, not me.* We simply will not let go of what we've built, and God will lovingly allow the above-ground man to crumble. The Gardener wants his trees always growing downward so they have the potential to grow upward and outward.

Blessed is the one who trusts in the LORD,
  whose confidence is in him.
They will be like a tree planted by the water
  that sends out its roots by the stream.
It does not fear when heat comes;
  its leaves are always green.
It has no worries in a year of drought
  and never fails to bear fruit.[6]

This is a picture of a man who is secure in God's love—rooted and established, as the Gardener desires. He sends out roots to find the supply of God's love. He is confident and at peace, no matter the pressures around him. His roots are deep and wide, always searching. The belowground work is not lagging behind the aboveground person but rather is feeding, informing, and fueling the healthy color and fruit above the ground in every success or storm. In God's Word, we see the X-ray of a healthy tree both below and above the ground:

The waters nourished it,
  deep springs made it grow tall;
their streams flowed
  all around its base
and sent their channels
  to all the trees of the field.
So it towered higher
  than all the trees of the field;
its boughs increased
  and its branches grew long,
  spreading because of abundant waters.
All the birds of the sky
  nested in its boughs,

all the animals of the wild
    gave birth under its branches;
all the great nations
    lived in its shade.
It was majestic in beauty,
    with its spreading boughs,
for its roots went down
    to abundant waters.[7]

Don't miss the connection between deep springs, base rooting, tall growth, and the abundance of life. Everything aboveground is made possible by what is happening below. One process nourishes and makes the other possible.

Nourished by God's love, we grow down to grow up and into Christ.

Be Built Up in Him Each Day

Rooted in love and established inwardly, we start building a new life in Christ. But how? Think about a first house or apartment that you need to move into and make livable. You start with the big stuff you need for daily existence, like a dining-room or kitchen table. A close second is a couch and maybe a few chairs for the living room, where people can relax or watch some TV. There is a natural priority system. You begin with furnishing your dwelling based on what is needed most, and then you build from there. Most people can't purchase everything they need right away, so they look to add the next thing that will make their home either more functional or more pleasing to be in. It's an ongoing process.

Your life, the Bible says, is like a house that God inhabits, which needs to be built up on a daily basis. You add to it to make it more effective, welcoming, and pleasing to God. Just like the home you live in, there is always a project that needs your attention. You are

God's dwelling, and in his mind, there is always a project or two or three to work on to add to his dwelling.

> Make every effort to add to your faith goodness; and to goodness, knowledge; and to knowledge, self-control; and to self-control, perseverance; and to perseverance, godliness; and to godliness, mutual affection; and to mutual affection, love. For if you possess these qualities in increasing measure, they will keep you from being ineffective and unproductive in your knowledge of our Lord Jesus Christ.[8]

This is the aboveground life the belowground rooting in God's love activates in the form of *following* Jesus each day. Whether you are a young Christian or a lifelong Christian isn't as important as following Christ on a daily basis. A yes to following Jesus is, by default, a no to building your life in other ways. When you build something, you need material to build with, and the quality of that material will determine the quality of what is built. Jesus tells us exactly how to build our lives in him every day, and what material we should rely on:

> These words I speak to you are not incidental additions to your life, homeowner improvements to your standard of living. They are foundational words, words to build a life on. If you work these words into your life, you are like a smart carpenter who built his house on solid rock. Rain poured down, the river flooded, a tornado hit—but nothing moved that house. It was fixed to the rock.
> But if you just use my words in Bible studies and don't work them into your life, you are like a stupid carpenter who built his house on the sandy beach. When a storm

rolled in and the waves came up, it collapsed like a house of cards.[9]

Solid security in the *love of God* produces solid application of the *words of God*.

Each man Jesus described chose to build a house, and the most important decision he had to make was what material he would use for the foundation. The house, like our tree, represents a life— your life and my life. It shouldn't be a hard choice to build a life well, and to build it on the words of God. But for so many men, what they know in their minds and hearts is difficult to accomplish in the big and small spaces of their lives. When a man fully comprehends God's love for him, he searches out and loves applying what God says. It's a "want to," not a "have to," because he is fully accepted, loved, and defined by God.

The opposite is also true. When a man is insecure and fearful and therefore questions God's love, he wavers in doing what God says. You can track it this way: *An area of insecurity in your life is an area where you won't apply God's Word.* If I fear that people won't accept me, I will do things that go against God's Word to be more accepted or visible. In fear, I start selfishly competing with others versus connecting with them. If I fear not having enough money at the end the month and doubt God's ability to provide, I will struggle with tithing or being generous. If I fear what other men think of me more than what God thinks of me, I will be less likely to share the love of God with them. Disobedience to God's ways in an area usually tracks with a fear connected to that area. If we aren't rooted in love, we live out of what we lack, and fear causes us to abandon God's direction. That isn't the Gardener's way for his planted ones.

Nourished by God's love, we build our lives daily in response to what God says.

Be Strong and Grow in Truth Each Day

When precious time is running out, we want to say and do things that matter. Nothing wasted. Shortly before his crucifixion, Jesus had this exact urgency for his disciples and was trying to provide the most clarity he could regarding their path forward and what following him would look like. He took great pains to assure them that while he might be physically absent, they would be in a process with him every day through God's Spirit, who had a specific purpose connected to their growth.

> "When he, the Spirit of truth, comes, he will guide you into all the truth. He will not speak on his own; he will speak only what he hears, and he will tell you what is yet to come. He will glorify me because it is from me that he will receive what he will make known to you. All that belongs to the Father is mine. That is why I said the Spirit will receive from me what he will make known to you."[10]

The process Jesus was describing is consistent with who he is and what spiritual dimension he operates in most powerfully— the dimension of truth. Jesus, in this same discussion, declared, "I am . . . the truth."[11] He meant that truth is God's intrinsic nature—an indispensable quality that determines his character, which informs everything he touches and relates to, including us. As his planted ones, we grow by taking into ourselves that essential force in God's nature—truth. If you are secure in God's love, the Bible says your relationship with truth will be growing. In fact, a growing comfort with truth develops where perhaps a previous fear of living in and working with truth existed. Secure in God's love, you can start to be more honest with God, more honest with yourself, and more truthful with others. Things that used to bring shame and that you used to hide no longer have power over you because of his love. Truth is not to be feared when you are secure in love.

> "This is the crisis we're in: God-light streamed into the world, but men and women everywhere ran for the darkness. They went for the darkness because they were not really interested in pleasing God. Everyone who makes a practice of doing evil, addicted to denial and illusion, hates God-light and won't come near it, fearing a painful exposure. But anyone working and living in truth and reality welcomes God-light so the work can be seen for the God-work it is."[12]

All truth is God's truth, and as my mentor J.P. has pounded into me over the years, "The truest thing about anything is what God says is true." What God says in the Bible is true. Jesus' life and example communicate truth. What the Holy Spirit speaks to us about God and his will is truth. Our present circumstances as they are versus what we hoped they would be is truth. In a relationship with the God of love and truth, reality is your friend. Interestingly, I find that most men who follow Jesus don't have trouble with God's truth about himself or even his will. Where they stumble and become insecure is when God tells them the truth *about themselves*. Something is pointed out to them that reflects the truth about who they really are versus some perception or image of themselves. This truth is the hardest truth to work with when you aren't rooted in God's love.

Enter fear and insecurity.

Men who are otherwise the most confident and assured people begin to make excuses. We justify, rationalize, and blame versus taking responsibility in the face of truth. God is trying to bring his truth, transform us, and grow us, and we don't even recognize it's him! Deep, insecure, and unhealed fears are still present, moving, and controlling our thoughts and actions. God is reflecting truth to us because he loves us, but we cannot humble ourselves before him in this way even though it's the safest place and the safest thing we could do. Fear separates God's love from God's truth that is coming to us, and instead of working with it, we deflect and avoid it.

Insecure men like the truth when it benefits them but loathe it when it exposes them. On the other hand, men secure in love seek, recognize, and respond to what is true regardless of the cost to their image or ego, because they know God's love is operating within truth and reality. More importantly, working with truth and reality is working with God!

"Whoever speaks on their own does so to gain personal glory, but he who seeks the glory of the one who sent him is a man of truth; there is nothing false about him."[13]

Nourished by God's love, we grow strong in truth by embracing and working with it.

Be Grateful Each Day

Fathers detect ingratitude like a shark can smell blood. Right, Dad? When children begin to assume they've authored all of their own blessings to the point of getting greedy, that's when a loving father will step in. Our heavenly father is no different. All good dads know that if their children don't possess an attitude of gratitude, all they have left to live out of will be *attitude*. Planted ones grow by gratitude, and not just when the seas are smooth, time is on our side, or the check is in the mail.

Be cheerful no matter what; pray all the time; thank God no matter what happens. This is the way God wants you who belong to Christ Jesus to live.[14]

An insecure man will trip over a no-matter-what-and-no-matter-what-happens attitude of gratitude. He believes the myth that God is absent in his adversity and present in his prosperity. An insecure man thinks that God's love isn't strong enough or deep enough to reach into the fire, be present in it, and forge a diamond out of it. In daily practice, we cultivate gratitude in the following ways:

- *Acknowledging God's presence.* "This is the day which the Lord has made; let's rejoice and be glad in it."[15]

- *Thanking God for challenges as well as blessings.* "It is good for me that I was afflicted, so that I may learn Your statutes."[16]

- *Thanking God that his character and love guide his timing.* "God has made everything beautiful for its own time. He has planted eternity in the human heart, but even so, people cannot see the whole scope of God's work from beginning to end."[17]

- *Sacrificially praising God in faith, even when we hurt.* "Therefore, let us offer through Jesus a continual sacrifice of praise to God, proclaiming our allegiance to his name."[18]

Fully identified with Christ's death and rooted in God's sacrificial love, we know that if God can create our salvation out of a crucifixion, he can certainly redeem the negatives of our lives for victorious and redeeming positives. The gospel proves it. That's how God wants us to think about him and live in him. God is at work in the pits as well as on the peaks of life. *No matter what,* we can thank him even though we may not be able to see a tangible reason for it in the moment. Planted ones thank God for all things in their lives, not just some things. There are no situational limitations for when God causes our cups to overflow. In fact, the counterintuitive moments of recognition and magnification of God's presence are the most meaningful and faith-filled.

> Even when I walk
> through the darkest valley,
> I will not be afraid,
> for you are close beside me.
> Your rod and your staff
> protect and comfort me.
> You prepare a feast for me
> in the presence of my enemies.
> You honor me by anointing my head with oil.
> My cup overflows with blessings.
> Surely your goodness and unfailing love will pursue me
> all the days of my life,
> and I will live in the house of the LORD
> forever.[19]

Nourished by God's love, we can overflow with gratefulness regardless of circumstance.

Invitation and Impartation

Repeated failures humble us and shake us inside.

These experiences, mingled with inner pride or fear, can cause us to retreat from opportunities to grow based on our past experiences and the perceptions we formed out of those difficult moments. That reality makes many men avoidant. That is, we attempt to make sure that we never again experience the same failure or trauma or anything else that is remotely similar. It's a defense mechanism. The irony is that by engaging in these defenses, we are actually recreating the very thing we're trying to avoid. Why is this important to recognize as we seek to live in God's acceptance?

Being secure in the love of God in Christ roots and secures us in life, but it isn't a final destination. God accepts and affirms us, but he loves us too much to leave us the way we are. So he invites us forward into new, nonavoidant growth.

> [Jesus says to us,] "Come to me. Get away with me and
> you'll recover your life. I'll show you how to take a real
> rest. Walk with me and work with me—watch how I
> do it. Learn the unforced rhythms of grace. I won't lay
> anything heavy or ill-fitting on you. Keep company with
> me and you'll learn to live freely and lightly."[20]

Walking and working. Learning and living. Not too threatening, is it?

It's reassuring when someone says, "I know how to do this, and I'll show you." There is nothing to fear, because we are rooted now. So what are we waiting for? Why the hesitation to go for what's next in our spiritual lives? Our marriage relationships? Our professional journeys? Our emotional development? God is with us, and he promises he isn't going anywhere.

I remember walking into a counselor's office with my wife, Chrissy. Our marriage was struggling because of my lack of maturity and fear of growth. More specifically, I was defensive and had a win-at-all-costs approach to resolving conflict. I was being avoidant, and God was calling me to new growth. I perceived disagreement as being put on trial versus discussing an issue. I could physically feel myself becoming defensive in a fight-or-flight sort of way when differences of opinion arose or when I was clearly wrong but couldn't own it. I personalized *everything*. I remember hoping I could overcome every wave welling up inside me before it crashed on the shore. Just like getting stuck in a large swell at the ocean, I was in between stages of maturity, not sure I would ever secure the peaceful, solid shores of intimacy. Better communication wasn't the issue. The problem went much deeper. Fixing Chrissy and her responses to me wasn't the issue either. Something inside me was afraid, but it manifested outwardly in prideful and harmful self-protection at all costs. Heck, I didn't like myself, but I was clearly unable to change my behavior on my own.

Mr. Have It All Together was being avoidant and needed counseling . . . bad.

I didn't know what the process would mean for me, and I feared there would be no way back once Pandora's box of my stuff was open. I had been so good at controlling the narrative and had argued so energetically. I defended myself, my way of thinking, and my actions. In the process, I had dug more than a few holes that seemingly would be hard to get out of. Those thoughts stoked fears, and those fears raised walls, and those walls were going to destroy my connection with my wife if I didn't find a way to move forward and grow. But God had been speaking to me in the proverbial "still small voice,"[21] which no one to this day has been able to explain. But I think that's the point. There are no formulas for when you're afraid, and some force inside you—a feeling, a peace, a needed level of confidence—arrives mysteriously in and around you and speaks.

"I got you," I sensed God say.

When you're insecure, those words can make you run faster away from the truth or help you face it. The tension needed a game-changing word, and that message was it. I knew it was from God. He was telling me that the belowground work had not been done, but he was going to help me do it so the whole life I had built above the ground could be saved. More assurance came:

"Don't panic. I'm with you.
    There's no need to fear for I'm your God.
I'll give you strength. I'll help you.
    I'll hold you steady, keep a firm grip on you."[22]

God was sending me a clear invitation to grow and, in that moment, imparted to me his love, presence, and promise to pursue growth without fear. Trust me, I had to send out roots to search for more of God's love to support the counseling process in Christ, but that year changed me and my marriage forever. Gone are the insecure and defensive blowouts. Present is a man who doesn't need to fear truth but will work with it *even if it concerns me*. Gone is a conflict avoider. Present is faith that believes that no matter what the outcome of the disagreement, God loves me and I will be just fine. In fact, that truth makes me calmer and more able to listen. Gone is the competitor who needs to win at all costs. Present is a desire not to lose my connection with God and with my wife. Gone is a guy that fears news or situations that involve delay, difficulty, loss, and even personal pain. Present is the understanding that God is not absent in my adversity, just as his purpose wasn't absent when Jesus was being crucified. This doesn't mean I welcome pain or suffering. It just means I know that because of God's love, nothing is ever fatal or final.

[Nothing] fazes us because Jesus loves us. I'm absolutely convinced that nothing—nothing living or dead, angelic or demonic, today or tomorrow, high or low, thinkable or unthinkable—absolutely *nothing* can get between us and God's love because of the way that Jesus our Master has embraced us.[23]

My marriage was reborn.

It was transformed as I grew up in God's love. It was being redeemed by his skilled and caring presence. It is being filled with ways to be that make me more of a man and less like a boy. Thanks to the Spirit of Truth, my marriage-scape is now full of more healthy days, moments, and intimacy. I get to cross off the list of things that bug and frustrate me "how my character flaws sabotage connection." My marriage angst is gone because I am now a spiritually and relationally motivated man. My past sins are behind me in Christ. In the end, God had a vision for me and my marriage: of what it could become if I became secure in his love and, in faith, used that rooting to grow me and my connection with Chrissy.

What about you? What part of the landscape of your life needs new growth to flow into it? What looks dead that needs God's breath and life? Whatever is coming to mind, just know this: Where you see death, God sees life.

Jesus extends to you his invitation to grow and the promise of his love imparted to you.

Maybe marriage isn't your "deadscape," where God's love is pushing you to suit up and show up. But there is a way to know what that area of your life is: Wherever the fear is, that is your area. And God's love in and through you wants to flow there. Wherever the angst is, that is your area. Wherever past failure has you paralyzed, that is your area. Wherever the repeated mistakes are located, that is your area. Wherever the destructive habit lies, that is your area. Wherever the risk feels great but the hope of reward is present, that is your area. Whatever harms your relationships with God and people, that is your area. Got it? Do you see it? Have you put a name to it? Now say yes to God's love.

You are rooted. You are being called forward. You will overflow with thanks.

"Forget the former things;
    do not dwell on the past.
See, I am doing a new thing!
    Now it springs up; do you not perceive it?
I am making a way in the wilderness
    and streams in the wasteland."[24]

Lord Jesus,

I come at your invitation. I seek an impartation of your love. I want your process because mine is not producing the fruit you seek. I need you to speak into the barren and dry places of my life. My roots are searching for you, for your love, for your care, and for your wisdom in this moment, because I want the new things you see that I don't. Forgive my neglect of your love filling my heart. Forgive my out-of-balance life in your love. Forgive my pursuit of activity in you over relationship with you. I surrender my vision of my life for yours. I surrender my hopes for your hopes. I surrender my dream of the life I thought I would live for the life your love is calling me to live. I reject the fears and lies that keep me from experiencing the new chapters you want to write in my life. I accept your offer of help. I receive the power and strength of the Holy Spirit for my next chapter. I declare my spiritual crucifixion so I can receive my spiritual resurrection. I am reaching down into your love to give me power to grow up into your vision. Thank you for calling me forward. Thank you for rooting me. Thank you for building me up. Thank you for growing *and strengthening me from the inside out. Thank you for the overflow of your love that is filling my heart right now. I praise and thank you for your commitment to finish your work in me. Cause me to flourish through your presence, so that your glory will be seen in me. In faith I pray in Jesus' name. Amen.*

8

SHOCK AND AWESOME

The Secure Risk and Go

I LIKE PREDICTABLE.

Knowing things *before the fact* helps me prepare. That's why I call my wife's girlfriends to get their take on potential anniversary or Christmas gifts for Chrissy. That's why I get recommendations and do research prior to traveling on vacation. That's why I would diligently assess a client's needs and work my inside contacts for information before a big meeting to win or keep an account. That's why I get second or third opinions before I let a surgeon take a scalpel to my flesh. Smart men get intel because knowledge before the fact is optimal. But here is the problem: We have to make most of our big decisions *before* the fact. The reality is, the best we can do is be persuaded or feel more assured that the decision is a good one, but we can't know our wives are going to love what we got them, know the recommended hot spot on vacation is fantastic, or know if the big meeting is going well until *after* the fact. After our wives get the gifts, after we try the food, and after we ask for the order and close the deal—*then* we know. But before that moment, the best we can hope for is to feel pretty good or very persuaded about going forward.

We simply have to go for it, confident and hopeful.

I felt really confident, for example, about my odds of reaching home after a night at Angel Stadium here in Southern California. It was a great night for baseball. The Angels won the game. We filed out of the parking lot. We hopped on familiar highways, took familiar freeway exits, made familiar turns, and expected a familiar outcome—getting home safely. Thirty years of experience on these same roads, tons of games under my belt, and a record of safely and securely pulling into my driveway at the end of the night persuaded me that this night would be no different. It's what I didn't know was happening while I was at the game that messed up my assumption about getting home safely. That space between feeling very persuaded and reality almost cost my wife and me our lives.

You see, what I didn't know was that a young woman was drinking with her friends in an apartment complex that night, and the complex was located near the same road I would be traveling later that evening at 10:45 p.m. I also didn't know that no one would warn her of the dangers of driving while intoxicated and persuade her to sleep it off or let someone *who wasn't drunk* drive her home. I also couldn't have predicted that she would leave the party, get in her car, turn on the ignition, put the car in drive, step on the gas, run a stop sign, and crash head-on into my car doing fifty-five miles per hour at exactly 10:45 p.m. I couldn't know what I couldn't know, but that didn't stop me from driving home from the game. I left the stadium *confident* and *persuaded*, and—in faith—I started home. But I couldn't *know* I would get home.

Faith is built into the very fabric of our daily existence. We see faith when we see two things happen: *a commitment before knowing* and *a completed action*. Remember that. In the real-life scenario I just described, and in many others, I commit before knowing, and I complete my faith by taking some action. I got in the car and started driving that fateful night. I get on a plane, and it takes off with me in it. I go to the doctor's office, I pick up my prescription at the pharmacy, and in faith I ingest the drug in hopes of getting some relief and healing. I'm willing to take certain physical or kinetic risks because the hope is strong enough or the objective means something to me. But I can never *know* before the fact with 100 percent certainty whether the outcome will be good.

My faith is exercised in the direction of my hope. "Faith is confidence in what we hope for and assurance about what we do not see."[1]

My youngest daughter taught me what that actually means.

"I'm with My Dad!"

When you're the youngest child, you grow up with a chip on your shoulder.

You're always chasing your older siblings' experiences and feel ripped off that you can't go where they go or do the things they do. You attempt to follow your siblings into their activities, and the answer they give you is "You can't come," or Mom and Dad say, "Sorry, sweetheart." There is an age, height, maturity, or danger factor blocking you from the fun your siblings are having, and it's beyond frustrating. No one likes being limited when there is adventure out there to be had—just ask the baby brother or sister of any family. That was true for me as the last of seven kids, and it's true of my youngest, Jenna. But on one particular occasion, my six-year-old daughter made a bold, improbable request, and it changed her life and *my life* forever.

We were in Mexico as a family, and our condominium was perched above the water and near a popular snorkeling spot. As boys will do, my son and I scoped out the property and quickly discovered a challenging opportunity. We found a cement platform jutting out from the top of a cliff, where, if we notched up our courage, we could take the plunge into the ocean. The drop was around forty feet, which may or may not sound high to you, but when I took a peek down to the ocean, it made me pause. I went first. Then my son went. Then we both went at the same time. Press repeat for a good hour. Thrilling, wet adventure. Oblivious to everything else at the time, I didn't realize that the baby of the family was watching, hoping, and moving behind the scenes to our jump-off point. Ryan had just jumped off the platform, and while I was waiting for him to clear the drop zone, I felt two strong pokes on my backside. What could that be?

Looking up at me in her mermaid goggles and matching swim-suit was Jenna.

She was clear: "Dad, I want to jump off with you and Ryan."

Instead of crushing her hopes with an immediate no, I decided to let her feel exactly what we felt when we looked over the edge. So I walked her over to see the literal depth of her request, believing she would feel the magnitude of it and then run back to the kiddie pool. To the edge we walked, she looked down, and then she looked up at me and nodded her head up and down, confirming to me that she was a go for Operation Flying Mermaid. I was still unconvinced, because I knew my daughter's tolerance for a physical risk like this was low. So I simply moved to Plan B: I switched my vocal setting to a fatherly baritone and began an ominous countdown.

"Ohhhhh-kay, Jenna. Heeeerrrre we go. I am going to count to three, and on three, we are going to jump aaaallllll the way down to the water. Here we go."

Deep breath. "Ooooonnne."

After I counted off, I looked down at her to check her resolve. She looked up at me with those mermaid goggles and nodded the go-ahead—up and down. I still thought her fear would rise up, and so in my lowest and most threatening tone, I bellowed, "Twooooo." Then I checked in again. Her eyes straight ahead, she squeezed my hand and squatted down, quadriceps flexed into the coiled position, ready to jump.

No fear in sight, so I paused for a safety speech. "Okay, Jenna, when I say three, we are going to jump together, but don't worry, I will have your hand. We are going to go deep into the water, but just kick your legs and swim to the top." Last safety check and the final nod of faith secure, I said, "Three."

Down. Down. Down. Me first. Then Jenna. Into the deep. She was up before me with a huge smile and couldn't get the words out fast enough: "That was fun, Dad. Let's do it again!"

What just happened? I was in shock and awe.

As we swam to the stairs to "do it again," I was reeling with confusion over what she had just done. She defied all the odds and surprised the biggest doubter of all—me! I never thought she would jump. Confused by her decision, I needed to know what happened, so halfway up the stairs, and before we jumped off the platform again, I stopped her.

"How did you do that? Weren't you scared?" I asked.

She started by confirming my suspicion. "I said to myself, 'I am really scared.'" What came next penetrated my soul. "But then I said to myself, 'I'm with my dad! And everything is going to be okay.' And then I jumped with you. C'mon, Dad. Let's go again!"

Jenna's lips were moving, but it was God talking through that simple and honest response. She couldn't know before the fact that this risk she was about to take would end well. But focused on me, strongly persuaded about me in her heart and mind, and secure in her view of me, she shocked her father, her brother, her mother, and her older sister. She believed I was big enough, strong enough, wise enough, and loving enough to make sure that she would be okay if she jumped off that cliff. I brought her to the edge—her eyes and heart were on me. I intentionally tried to scare her off and tap into her six-year-old fear—her eyes and heart were rooted in me. I presented the moment to her and a last chance to abandon her hope—she reacted with confidence and put her body in the ready position. She was with her father, and in her mind, she was convinced, *Everything is going to be okay.* Her faith in me was proved that day.

So what did God speak to me?

"Your life in me will never be greater than your view of me."

For Jenna, that day was a day of seeing things she had never seen before. That day was about doing things she had never done before. That day was about feeling things she had never felt before. That day was about overcoming major fears and allowing faith in her father to take inner control. How did all that take place? What made that kind of personal risk-taking possible? What inner process occurred? What clicked for her? And how do I overcome the fears that keep me from seeing the promises of God realized in my life? What's the lesson?

Among the many lessons here is one you can take away right now: When we're secure in our Father, when we're convinced in our inner being of his love, when we're assured of his character, and when we're persuaded of his trustworthiness, we can say goodbye to fear and hello to our deepest hopes.

That day in Mexico, I witnessed and participated in the single greatest faith lesson of my life as Jenna committed without knowing and completed her faith by taking an action. That preaches to me. That day and moment, God pulled me in tight and whispered, *"You are secure in me. You can be fearless with me."*

My response?

I repented.

It was all in the mix that day as God used Jenna's faith in action to show me how I need to think about him, his love for me, his care for me, his ability, his character, and his trustworthiness. Fully accepted, fully loved, fully defined, and fully rooted in his love, I am free to jump into all his purposes for me and start living the adventure he has for me. More personally, he wants to see me live that way!

"My righteous one will live by faith.
    And I take no pleasure
    in the one who shrinks back."

But we do not belong to those who shrink back and are destroyed, but to those who have faith and are saved.[2]

When I have God's promise and God's acceptance, I am persuaded to move toward my strongest hopes. No shrinking back. Every day we take risks for the future we seek, and it isn't about how much faith we put out; it's about where we have placed our faith.

I'm building experiences of faith that keep persuading me to risk more for God's will in my life whenever he gives me a direction to go in or he makes a promise for me to believe in. The real test of my relationship with God is when I can't know before the fact if what I'm about to do in him will end well. But . . .

"I'm with my dad! And everything is going to be okay."

Persuaded he loves me, I risk.

Here We Go!

Every man who loves God will find his back against the wall.

For those who know the width, the height, the length, and the depth of his love, God will steadily test our view of him to deliver more life in him. We'll find ourselves with our backs against the wall and hear questions like . . .

- Are you going to trust me?
- Did I call you out of the world?
- What does my Word say?
- What shows love for me?
- What did Jesus model?
- Have I ever failed you?
- Is your future in my hands?
- What have you got to lose?
- Am I enough?
- What is my promise to you?
- Am I with you or not?

The progression from insecurity to maturity in the Father's love and acceptance is a progression of risk. Jesus says, *"Come and see. See how much I love you."* Then he says, *"Come and commit. Commit to grow up and into me—deep roots below supporting the life aboveground."* And as we live out of his love and demonstrate more open commitment, he will make a third invitation: *"Come and die. Completely throw off fear and start aggressively advancing my purposes and trusting me everywhere and in every way you possibly can."*

Fresh risks need to be taken. Old risks we took in the past have had their moment. Our view of God is being tested now, and that means we need to take new risks. Our identity is settled.

Our energy is renewed. Our expression is imminent. Our King is calling us forward now.

Spiritual cliff after spiritual cliff, opportunity after opportunity to trust God will be presented to us. It is the journey of faith, and when we are with our Father and are remaining in his love, the cliffs in our lives are progressively confronted and conquered. Each time we jump off, trusting his presence and promise, God proves himself to be who he says he is—faithful. And with each experience, the things we used to fear greatly are now more like speed bumps in our spiritual journeys—we feel them, but they don't stop our movement forward. Why? Because we *know*, at the deepest level in our spirits, that God isn't present in some things and absent in others. He is present in all things, at all times, in all circumstances, and we risk entering all of these arenas persuaded of his presence and holding fast to a promise. The deep working of love and acceptance causes our spiritual courage to rise as God says, *"Go ahead. I am with you."* God used a munchkin girl to tower over my fear, and her message from God to me is now God's message to you.

What's next for you? God is calling you to RISK in specific ways that involve four key characteristics:

Right views of God
A settled identity
A sacrificial mindset
Kingdom faith

A Secure Man Has a Right View of God

God's man, rooted and secure in God's love, understands that his life in God will never outperform his view of God. If God is big to him, he will believe big, love big, and risk big in the direction of his hope. Keeping God who he says he is versus who our fears try to make him is spiritual warfare. To stay secure—keeping God big and risking big—we must never let our view of him be anything less than what he has declared about himself. He doesn't like our fears turning him into someone he is not. Nobody does.

God's Message:
"Don't let the wise brag of their wisdom.
    Don't let heroes brag of their exploits.
Don't let the rich brag of their riches.
    If you brag, brag of this and this only:
That you understand and know me.
    I'm GOD, and I act in loyal love.
I do what's right and set things right and fair,
    and delight in those who do the same things.
These are my trademarks."[3]

Going forward in faith, our eyes are fixed on God as he truly is.

A Secure Man Has a Settled Identity

A man fully defined by Christ's act of love is sure about who he is and what he is called to be and do. He is dead to sin. He is alive to God. He has access to God. He has authority in God. Living out his truest identity produces real integrity, creates strong liberty, drives his best energy, and ensures a solid legacy. Not only does this sound good, but it's rooted in a fundamental truth: When you know who you are, *you know what to do.*

What power and freedom there is in this! When you know who you are in God's love, you exercise *more faith.* You commit. You act on God's commands and promises. You battle to work out what God has worked into you through his love. You stay rooted in him, and you fight the good fight. That means living a lifestyle of saying no to temptation so you can say yes to God.

You take hold of who you are and refuse to let go. And you never give yourself permission to take a vacation from who you are. That's a man of God.

> But you, man of God, flee from [temptation], and pursue
> righteousness, godliness, faith, love, endurance and
> gentleness. Fight the good fight of the faith. Take hold of
> the eternal life to which you were called when you made
> your good confession in the presence of many witnesses.[4]

Because we know who we are as men of God, we fight for faith. We take risks in the direction of our strongest hopes in God. Our helmet of salvation is secure, our shield of faith is up, and our hand is on the hilt of the blade—God's promise.

Our inner man is locked down. Here we go!

A Secure Man Has a Sacrificial Mindset

Loving God and people isn't about feeling up to it. If that were the case, Jesus would have taken a pass on the whole torture and crucifixion thing. Powerful feelings are present in every man. But they need not control what happens next. Secure in God's love, the man of God finds himself saying no to feelings and yes to his faith when pressure to compromise is present. He chooses to sacrifice, giving up himself for God and others in order to take up his higher allegiance. His model is Christ. He knows the crucified life precedes a resurrection life. His outer man is being broken as his inner man is growing strong. His mindset reflects the risk-filled prayer, "Not my will, but yours be done,"[5] and he means it. He is ready to pay a price to stay faithful to God and redeem situations for God's purposes. He will drop what he is doing. He will empty his wallet. He will put aside his agenda. He will put others first. He will go when other men won't. He will step in. He will bring justice to a moment. He will serve anyone. His body is not his own. His sacrifice is his worship. This is you!

> I plead with you to give your bodies to God because of all he has done for you. Let them be a living and holy sacrifice—the kind he will find acceptable. This is truly the way to worship him.[6]

Going forward, we choose to lay down our lives. No one tells us to.

A Secure Man Has a Kingdom Faith

A Kingdom man lives in a different dimension than other men. He is on a mission. He is an ambassador. He represents Christ in the world. He advances God's agenda. He has limited time. He has an unknown ending. He has a scheduled meeting with his King when his service on earth has timed out. He knows he was created with intention to do the works God has prepared uniquely for him to do. There is a responsibility that comes with bestowed authority. He is a citizen of heaven. As a servant of the King, he belongs to no man but makes himself the servant of every man so that he can win every man. He enters a long line of servants who came before him; he is under their same commission, operating under the same power, and possesses the same set of keys that unlock evil gates and loose God's Kingdom power and agenda wherever he walks.

> [Jesus said to Simon,] "And I tell you that you are Peter, and on this rock I will build my church, and the gates of Hades will not overcome it. I will give you the keys of the kingdom of heaven; whatever you bind on earth will be bound in heaven, and whatever you loose on earth will be loosed in heaven."[7]

"This, then, is how you should pray:

"'Our Father in heaven,
hallowed be your name,
your kingdom come,
your will be done,
    on earth as it is in heaven.'"[8]

We belong to God's rule. We advance his realm. We take eternal risks. We have concluded that a safe spiritual life is a wasted Kingdom life.

Against All Hope

Every man who loves God will find himself alone in his faith.

When God says to do something, he doesn't say that everyone is going to agree with you and love you for it. In fact, so many times the opposite is true. I think of 2020. It was the year of COVID and the nationwide unrest sparked by the officer-involved public murder of George Floyd in Minneapolis. At the outset of these events, no one knew how long, how serious, how political, or how overshadowing they would be to our existence and way of life. The operative word for me and so many millions was *crazy*. It was a crazy year to be a human being, an American, and a follower of Jesus, thrust into the middle of a historical and cultural hurricane. These two events tested our inner substance, revealed our truest sources of identity, and exposed our gods as a culture.

At the outset of the COVID crisis, my state was one of the first to have a mandatory quarantine—California was going completely indoors. No one knew, at the time, if that was the right thing to do. When my own personal quarantine order came down, I felt strongly that quarantining would spread from the

West Coast and head east across the Mississippi River, until the whole nation was binging on Netflix, working from home, and buying toilet paper on eBay. I remember calling my producer for the *Every Man* livestream and saying, "I think we need to stop our current series, pivot, and create a series for men globally called *The Corona Chronicles*, talking to God's people about God's plan in the midst of crazy. He thought I was crazy, but God kept telling me that more men would be working from home and would be able to watch. It was a total gamble, and I went all out to raise awareness. I didn't have graphics, messages, or descriptions to get out the word. My wonderful team at Every Man Ministries rallied, and we launched the seven-week series nationwide. This series ended up reaching more than one hundred thousand men around the world and increased our livestream audience by a factor of forty.

God was leading, and I jumped off. Here we go!

On May 25, 2020, news broke of the officer-involved murder of George Floyd, sending the country into nationwide protests, riots in most large cities, and an overpoliticized news cycle. COVID took a back seat for the next month as the national dialogue pivoted around race. In much the same way, there was a need for prophetic and clear teaching in the midst of this that didn't drift into the cultural and political movements that hijacked such a serious issue. I invited friends of mine who are black pastors to join me for a discussion on race and a new series called *I Can't Breathe*. In the highly charged political and cultural moment, there were reactions across the board from negative to positive. Once again the audience swelled, and more people were reached. A clarion call went forth to engage compassion and extend Jesus' love to those who were hurting during this time. I lost many friends and fellow brothers in the cultural and political aftermath for simply talking about what God's heart was and elevating the example of

Jesus within his own time and culture by using the parable of the good Samaritan.

Here we go in faith again.

I wasn't looking to cable news for my direction. I wasn't looking to a political party. I wasn't naively pumping energy into any left-wing or right-leaning movements. In fact, I fasted from cable news. I doubled up in prayer. I sought the Lord. I took advantage of the promised and present Holy Spirit inside of me. I searched God's Word for his heart in this moment. I looked at the example of Jesus. I studied the parable of the good Samaritan and let Jesus ask me the ultimate question: *"Who is your neighbor?"* I leaned into my close friends who were African American, and we worked together to bring perspective and prophetic insight from God's Word to a super-tough time for black Americans. Even still, I was misunderstood, criticized, and labeled.

So was Jesus. And you will be too.

Blessed are those who are persecuted because of
   righteousness,
      for theirs is the kingdom of heaven.

Blessed are you when people insult you, persecute you
and falsely say all kinds of evil against you because of
me. Rejoice and be glad, because great is your reward in
heaven, for in the same way they persecuted the prophets
who were before you.[9]

When we see Jesus operate in his time, we see him plop in the middle of a culture that was filled with ethnic division, political division, and religious division, with each movement jockeying for visibility and power. What did he do? He walked alone, reaching out to those who felt marginalized within their culture amid all the tension. He broke the rules to reach out to the ethnically, morally, physically, and socially marginalized to let them know they were not alone. No more, no less. He didn't start an organization; he went to these marginalized people. He left the ninety nine he very easily could have hung out with—they were a familiar fraternity. And instead, he went to comfort those who were suffering and felt isolated, hurt by factors beyond their control, or lonely in that moment in time. Secure in the Father's love, he told the world that he would go to the downtrodden, and under pressure, he did it.

[Jesus said,]

"God's Spirit is on me;
   he's chosen me to preach the Message of good news
      to the poor,
Sent me to announce pardon to prisoners and
   recovery of sight to the blind,
To set the burdened and battered free,
   to announce, 'This is God's time to shine!'"[10]

So often his own disciples, stuck in the broken mentality of male culture, would watch him operate and ask themselves, *What is he doing with those people? What is he doing with her? Why won't he take on Rome? Why is he being so disruptive with his associations? What's he doing hanging around on that side of town? Why does he intentionally seek out people we avoid?* Secure in the Father's acceptance, Jesus didn't need man's approval, and so he kept on fulfilling his mission of bringing God's love and justice to everybody who was left out. He took the hits, but it didn't knock him off his mark. He did think it was a bit humorous, though.

[Jesus said,] "John came neither eating nor drinking, and they say, 'He has a demon.' The Son of Man came eating and drinking, and they say, 'Here is a glutton and a drunkard, a friend of tax collectors and sinners.' But wisdom is proved right by her deeds."[11]

Sometimes you just can't win, except in God. Is your back to the wall because of culture? Are you feeling alone in your faith position? Stay persuaded. Stay convinced. Stay consistent in your truest identity. Stay committed to the heart of the Father and the example of the Son. Stay filled with his Spirit and reject the spirit of the culture that tries to hijack the mission. You might be misunderstood, but you'll be fine. You're in good company. Against all hope, you need to keep risking, keep believing, and keep letting God be big. If you're looking for inspiration and a model for total inner security while standing all alone, be like Abraham. He had his good and bad moments, but the good moment God commended him for was *really good*. He stood so tall, God decided to make him the "father of faith."

Abraham showed all men of faith how to believe and behave when the chips are down and we have to make a choice between what we see, how we feel, and what our faith is calling us to.

Against all hope, Abraham in hope believed and so became the father of many nations, just as it had been said to him, "So shall your offspring be." Without weakening in his faith, he faced the fact that his body was as good as dead—since he was about a hundred years old—and that Sarah's womb was also dead. Yet he did not waver through unbelief regarding the promise of God, but was strengthened in his faith and gave glory to God, being fully persuaded that God had power to do what he had promised. This is why "it was credited to him as righteousness." The words "it was credited to him" were written not for him alone, but also for us, to whom God will credit righteousness—for us who believe in him who raised Jesus our Lord from the dead.[12]

Did you catch it? Abraham had a promise from God, and he was "fully persuaded." So what did he do? He committed without knowing the outcome. He approached his bride and said, "Here goes nothing, babe. We are making a baby!" I think this is one of the most humorous, human, and hope-filled scenes in all of Scripture. Can't you just see Sarah saying, "Okay, babe! God promised us a child, so I suppose we're going to have to take some action! I believe!" Then can't you see Abraham saying, "What a woman!" This is the scene. This is the man. This is the model. This is our spiritual mentor for staying secure *in the moment*. Scripture says this is the road map to pleasing God—committing without knowing when God gives a promise.

God says, "That's what my guys do, and I love it."

Here we go!

Heavenly Father,

I know that you are calling me forward to an edge—my edge—a new experience in faith. You're asking me to trust you before the fact and step off into the unknown. Your love has never failed me, and there is no reason to doubt now. So, because of who you are, I am putting my hand in yours. I sense through your Word and my circumstances that it's time to act on the one thing I am most cautious about in my walk with you. You are calling me into the unknown just as you called Abraham into uncharted waters, directions, and steps of faith that showed him it was all you. That's the kind of faith I want, and those are the steps I'm ready to take—the uncharted ones. I know that you have a direction for me. I know you have given me your great promises to assure me. Now there is only one thing left to do— complete my faith in you with action. This is for me alone to do. Amen.

Use this space to write down the specific way God is calling you forward in faith, and the spiritual risk you will now take based on his revealed will and promise to you.

9

THROWING OPEN THE DOORS

The Secure Relate

VULNERABLE. That is the best word to describe how I was feeling before having the scariest conversation of my short life. I was twenty-one. Ahead of me was a great future with an amazing woman. Behind me, though, was a past she deserved to know about. So, yes, I felt extremely vulnerable, intentionally opening myself to the possibility that a misadventure in truth telling would be a deal breaker for Chrissy. Thoughts were swirling. Would this be a relationship killer? The end of a dream I thought was from God? The only sure thing in all of this was that the relationship was moving fast, and it was clear that she was as serious about me as I was about her.

That reality created a new demand of character: transparency. Not my strong suit. Like any man, I had layers—some known and some unknown. At this point in the relationship and because I respected her more than any girl I had ever met, Chrissy deserved to know my *whole* story, not just the latest chapters of my journey. These recent faith chapters were the ones that drew her to me—the ones that involved a man being completely reshaped and repurposed by God's love. And now, in a strange twist, that guy—the new one God had made more secure—felt led to put himself in the awkward position of possibly losing her out of a need to be transparent.

Enter Spencer Tang.

Spence was one of my closest friends and confidants at UCLA. I needed a second opinion and was secretly hoping he would give me a great faith-based reason not to open up to Chrissy. You know—a back door. A release valve. A solution that involved having her best interests in mind. So on one of our regular beach-volleyball days in Santa Monica, I decided to hijack a break in the action. I got my courage up and revealed to him what I was thinking about doing.

Me: So things are getting pretty serious with Chrissy and me.

Spencer: I know, dude, because I hardly see you anymore! Seriously, though, she is awesome.

Me: So there is one thing I need your advice on.

Spencer: For sure, bro. What's going on?

Me: Okay, so here goes. Chrissy doesn't know about me before I became a Christian. Sexually, I mean. She knows I was Life of the Party guy in my senior class. She knows about all the changes God has made in my life. She knows I love Jesus now. She sees the new me. But she doesn't know that I'm not a virgin. I haven't gone there. Even though it was only a one-time thing with one girl my senior year, I haven't gotten the courage up to put that on the table.

Spencer: So what are you going to do?

Me: I know it's important to her that she marry a virgin, because she has kept herself for marriage. So I feel like I need to tell her that I'm not.

Spencer: You gotta tell her, bro. You owe it to her. Yah, you gotta do it. If you love her, you will definitely tell her.

Me (*after a very deep breath*): That's what I thought you'd say. It's time. I feel like this is what God wants. We have a date this Friday, and I'll just tell her the facts.

End scene. Fast-forward three days. New scene. Friday night with Chrissy.

We're at the same beach in almost the exact same spot where I sat with Spencer just a few days before. On the drive down Santa Monica Boulevard, I act as if everything is okay, pretend like this is just another date, but my acting skills start to falter the second we lay a blanket on the beach. I start shaking physically, and it's obvious to Chrissy that something is wrong.

"What's the matter? Are you okay?" She rubs my back to comfort me.

It has all come down to this moment of truth, and I'm speechless. I can't get it out. So what comes next? Tears. That's right. Tears. Little streaks start rappelling down my face like a unit of army rangers rappelling off a cliff. The tears just keep falling. This is bad. Now she is really concerned.

"What is it? Talk to me," she says.

Big, deep breath. It all comes down to this. *God, help me.*

"So the person that you met this year is a new person," I begin. "You met the new Kenny. But there is one part of my life that I haven't told you about that you deserve to know about, because I know it's important to you."

"What is it?" she asks.

The facts start to flow about a fateful night my senior year in high school. Call it what you want. An admission. A confession. An exercise in transparency. It feels like stupidity, but the truth is going to be told—no secrets. Spencer's words are spurring me on: *"You gotta tell her, bro. You owe it to her. Yah, you gotta do it. If you love her, you will definitely tell her."*

I am still shaking. I'm a mess. My voice is cracking. It takes about five minutes but feels like an eternity. Chrissy is a person of conviction. Dread and doubt are spreading, so I stop the narrative, which opens the door to what must happen next: her response.

In this moment, fear is compelling me to defend myself. I want to make excuses. I want to overspiritualize things. But God won't let me. I am totally exposed. I'm so nervous, I have to stand up to breathe and brace myself. I can only stare straight ahead at the setting sun and wonder if it's a metaphor for what is about to happen in this relationship. A massive source of light, life, and comfort retreating into darkness.

No response. Chrissy is processing.

Then she stands up and says, "Look at me." She steps toward me and repeats herself, *"Look at me."* She takes another step closer, less than an inch away. No words at first. She wants to make sure I am seeing her. Then she wraps her arms around my waist. She pulls me close to her body. I look down at her and brace myself. Am I staring into those piercing green eyes for the last time?

She lowers the hammer.

"When I met you, I was not meeting that person. I met a new person. I also would never have known or thought anything different about you because of how God has changed your life and who you are right now. I hope, from now on, you feel free."

Vulnerable has now officially turned to *freedom*.

No fear.

Intentional Abandon

"I hope, from now on, you feel free."

When fear is eliminated from any relationship, and full acceptance replaces it, a shift in that relationship occurs. A safety and security enter that allow two people to relate on a different, more open, and transparent level. What once polluted, clouded, or could potentially sabotage the relationship is not a factor any longer. Where fear makes a man guarded, self-protective, and withdrawn in various ways, love and acceptance that are believed and felt create a new willingness to trust and pursue the connection. No hiding of self. No hiding your connection. No holding back. Assured people want the relationship to be fully seen and the association to be fully known. Something new is about to happen. The old rules no longer apply.

You put yourself *out there*.

When one of the Pharisees invited Jesus to have dinner with him, he went to the Pharisee's house and reclined at the table. A woman in that town who lived a sinful life learned that Jesus was eating at the Pharisee's house, so she came there with an alabaster jar of perfume. As she stood behind him at his feet weeping, she began to wet his feet with her tears. Then she wiped them with her hair, kissed them and poured perfume on them.

When the Pharisee who had invited him saw this, he said to himself, "If this man were a prophet, he would know who is touching him and what kind of woman she is—that she is a sinner."[1]

Intelligent and intentional abandon toward God follows the death of fear and the arrival of God's pervasive love and acceptance.

What the world, religion, culture, materialism, social capital, titles, visibility, and every other false fountain of meaning cannot do, Jesus does. He eliminates the acceptance issue. He fully defines you. He fully dignifies you as his own. You know who you are. You know whose you are. You have nothing to prove to anyone. You are rooted below. You are growing strong and reaching toward heaven above. You are risking anew for him. You are complete. More importantly, you have processed this with both your head and your heart. It has been internalized. You have been rooted and established in God's love. You have been made new, and the effect of this strengthening in your inner man is a fearlessness and public willingness to express your gratitude and love back to God. No one can see or understand fully all that has happened inside you, but your world will know. A release is seen.

This is what Jesus hopes for but doesn't always experience with his people. The woman who sought out Jesus in the account we just read was transformed and was about to give a lesson to men not yet locked down in their inner man. Having internalized God's love and acceptance, the transformed and uninvited woman now endangered herself *in front of men* to fearlessly worship Christ. The only buffer saving her from an undignified and immediate removal from the room was Jesus himself. Why did these men want to get rid of her? Because in everyone's mind except one, her actions were wrong on every level—culturally, socially, morally, and religiously. She was an object of criticism. She was already judged. She was making things tense, even awkward, for all who were spectating at that moment. She was creating issues for Jesus in the minds of the men. She was vulnerable. The irony in the midst of all this broken male energy is that they were assessing and perceiving the situation all wrong in the mind of God. Jesus told the men that this woman had just taken them to school.

What was wrong in their minds was beyond right in Christ's.

Jesus answered [his dinner host], "Simon, I have something to tell you."

"Tell me, teacher," he said.

"Two people owed money to a certain moneylender. One owed him five hundred denarii, and the other fifty. Neither of them had the money to pay him back, so he forgave the debts of both. Now which of them will love him more?"

Simon replied, "I suppose the one who had the bigger debt forgiven."

"You have judged correctly," Jesus said.

Then he turned toward the woman and said to Simon, "Do you see this woman? I came into your house. You did not give me any water for my feet, but she wet my feet with her tears and wiped them with her hair. You did not give me a kiss, but this woman, from the time I entered, has not stopped kissing my feet. You did not put oil on my head, but she has poured perfume on my feet. Therefore, I tell you, her many sins have been forgiven—as her great love has shown. But whoever has been forgiven little loves little."[2]

Big acceptance through big forgiveness produces reckless love for God.

Big lesson? The secure relate to God fearlessly. Those who are loved much love Jesus back much. They are public. They are proud. They want him to see their association with him. They want him to know their gratitude. If you happen to be present and watching it transpire, you're in the presence of authentic intimacy between two people. The woman used to be afraid that all was going to be lost; then Jesus stepped in closer to accept, love, forgive, and embrace her, saying, *"I hope, from now on, you feel free.*

We're good. There is no separation now or ever. You can't lose me, but now you can focus on enjoying, interacting with, appreciating, and pleasing me with your worship."

No need to hold back *anything*.

> By entering through faith into what God has always wanted to do for us—set us right with him, make us fit for him—we have it all together with God because of our Master Jesus. And that's not all: We throw open our doors to God and discover at the same moment that he has already thrown open his door to us. We find ourselves standing where we always hoped we might stand—out in the wide open spaces of God's grace and glory, standing tall and shouting our praise.[3]

Set right. Doors thrown open. Standing in pure hope. Shouting praise. This describes the woman Jesus affirmed and defended. This describes the person who has internalized who Jesus is and what his love means. This describes what God hopes will describe us. But is it me? Is it you? Do we still care about the optics when it comes to our relationship with Jesus? Or, secure in his acceptance and approval, do we let out the energy and appreciation the place of grace demands? Do we intelligently and intentionally bring to Jesus that reckless love and adoration that spill onto all who see us? Is our freedom in his presence challenging fear-filled and insecure restraint? Do we care anymore about the rules of decorum before the Man who loved us enough to die for us? Or do we abandon routine and stale worship for something real and authentic? Do people who truly love one another celebrate that love publicly and openly? What do people see when they see you in his presence? What is your response when you encounter your Savior, the one true Lover of your soul?

No water or tears? No kisses? No oil?

Our personal, emotional, and physical responses to Jesus' love and acceptance matter to him, as we see from the encounter with the "sinful" woman and his chastisement of the men who were *supposed* to be close to him. What did Jesus want men to see and imitate from this object lesson? Gleaning directly from what happened, we can say confidently that the inner security created by Christ's love produces an outer freedom to relate to him, associate ourselves with him, energetically appreciate him, and confidently love him back without care or concern about who is in the room. The greatly loved *greatly love Jesus back* in multiple, varied, and above all, personal dimensions. Why above all? Because relationships are personal! Jesus' love must be personal to us. Personal means not distant. Personal means intimate. Personal means that in this relationship, we can risk being vulnerable. We can be defenseless and not be hurt. There is potential injury from others, but Jesus protects and supports us. Personal means unguarded and abandoned, unafraid to give all of ourselves instead of just parts of ourselves. It's personal now, and in a strange twist, the loved person—the new one made secure by God—feels led to put himself in the awkward position of possibly losing the approval of men to gain a true connection with God. For a man, that personal decision looks and sounds a lot like this:

> The very credentials these people are waving around as
> something special, I'm tearing up and throwing out with
> the trash—along with everything else I used to take credit
> for. And why? Because of Christ. Yes, all the things I
> once thought were so important are gone from my life.
> Compared to the high privilege of knowing Christ Jesus
> as my Master, firsthand, everything I once thought I had
> going for me is insignificant—dog dung. I've dumped

it all in the trash so that I could embrace Christ and be embraced by him.[4]

Set in love. Doors thrown open. Firm in hope. A reckless embrace. You and Jesus. This is the shift God wants.

Receivers Are Responsible

Insecurity robs our energy—from God and others.

We spend so much time wondering, speculating, worrying, and trying to predict what will happen, what people will think, and what everything is going to mean for us that we become self-absorbed. By default, the self-absorbed man thinking self-absorbed thoughts and making self-absorbed choices channels all his energy inward to the benefit of, you guessed it, *self*. The big losers in his life are others who need him to make the transition from looking inward—looking out for self—to seeing them. They wonder when, for God's sake, he will be able to say no to himself and yes to the needs of others. Meanwhile, millions of needs around the world, big and small, remain unmet each day because they elude the detection and interest of the insecure man who is watching out for himself.

The result? God's love and justice fail to arrive in others' lives.

The world is desperately waiting for a certain man. A man who has been relieved of most forms of anxiety. A man who has been inwardly recalibrated. A man who is fiercely comfortable with being a giver instead of a taker. A man who can break the rules in a strong way for the sake of others. A man whose strength, power, and influence aren't questioned, because they're guided by equally strong compassion and character. A man who possesses peace that springs forth from a river of confidence that intuitively runs toward the presence of need. A man who not only knows who

God is but is fully defined by him, by his Word, by his example, and by his mercies toward him. A man who is self-forgetful. Why do people need that man? Because the insecure kind—the ones working out their fears of insignificance and a lack of worth—abuse, neglect, and exploit them. That's why. You know men like that. You know the type well. Men living out of what they lack. That used to describe *you*.

But now? You express your experience.

The kingdom of heaven is like a king who wanted to settle accounts with his slaves. And when he had begun to settle them, one who owed him ten thousand talents was brought to him. But since he did not have the means to repay, his master commanded that he be sold, along with his wife and children and all that he had, and repayment be made. So the slave fell to the ground and prostrated himself before him, saying, "Have patience with me and I will repay you everything." And the master of that slave felt compassion, and he released him and forgave him the debt.[5]

Distressed and vulnerable turns to released and free. This is an epic turnaround!

King and slave. Creditor and debtor. Authority and vulnerability. Massive burden and minuscule resources. Irresistible forces and immovable realities. There *should have been* only one conclusion, one response, and one outcome. A bad one for the slave. And yet compassion and mercy intervened to bring peace to the distress and security where there was vulnerability. Let's give it to the slave. That was a phenomenal performance. Falling to the ground and prostrating himself before the king. The reverence, the speech, and the sincerity behind the promise. The award-winning, heart-wrenching honesty was so compelling that a powerful king saw it, felt compassion, then lavished grace, rescuing this drowning man's life and dignity. Not the outcome we expected. It was a complete head-to-heart process for the king. Compassion replaced condemnation. Freedom replaced bondage for the slave. But did this experience of mercy that lavished so much peace, relief, and assurance on the slave create the desired turnaround within him?

> But that slave went out and found one of his fellow slaves who owed him a hundred denarii; and he seized him and began to choke him, saying, "Pay back what you owe!" So his fellow slave fell to the ground and began to plead with him, saying, "Have patience with me and I will repay you." But he was unwilling, and went and threw him in prison until he would pay back what was owed.[6]

When Jesus told the story of the debtor to explain the actions of the sinful woman, the focus was on how an encounter with love and mercy changes forever how forgiven people relate to God. That is, we don't hold back how we feel. We are fearless in our worship and care little about what others see or think. We make ourselves vulnerable before others to express our affection toward God.

When Jesus told the rest of the story of the debtor, the focus was on how our encounter with God's love should change how forgiven people *relate to others*. The focus of the king wasn't how the slave related to him but how the slave related to others *after* the king forgave the debt and made him whole. Specifically, did the receiver of mercy and compassion reproduce the same mercy and compassion toward others in his life? The king strongly expected that this slave, having been made secure through the

king's compassion, would likewise express his experience by showing compassion toward others in his life. The slave was exposed
and vulnerable. The king chose mercy. The slave, on the other
hand? He was forgiven a billion-dollar debt, and yet he choked
his fellow slave and debtor for less a few thousand dollars! When a
grace-receiving debtor became an unforgiving destroyer, it wasn't
only deeply disappointing to the king; it boiled his blood. Did you
catch how Jesus described the ungrateful slave?

He was "unwilling." Unwilling to pay forward the experience
he just had with the king. Unwilling to reproduce what he had
received. Unwilling to allow an encounter with compassion and
mercy to define how he would treat others in the future. The slave
was glad to be debt free, but the encounter failed to touch his
heart, character, and conduct. That unwillingness to freely give
away what he had so freely received ruined his relationship with
others and brought forth a second, and most uncomfortable,
encounter with the king.

> So when his fellow slaves saw what had happened, they
> were deeply grieved and came and reported to their
> master all that had happened. Then summoning him, his
> master said to him, "You wicked slave, I forgave you all
> that debt because you pleaded with me. Should you not
> also have had mercy on your fellow slave, in the same way
> that I had mercy on you?" And his master, moved with
> anger, handed him over to the torturers until he would
> repay all that was owed him. My heavenly Father will also
> do the same to you, if each of you does not forgive his
> brother from your heart.[7]

Those who receive anything from God are responsible to
reproduce the same actions in their relationships. That is God's

intention. That is the King's expectation. But more importantly, that is the result of our transformation and rooting in God's love. Whatever the perceived loss in giving of ourselves, we can let it go because God's love transforms loss into gain. Whatever the wound or trauma that seems unforgivable, it is forgivable because God forgave us.

However different someone may be from you, remember that you were a stranger and alien to God before Christ, and he accepted and received you. You have had an encounter with a generous, loving, forgiving, and encouraging King who has a simple expectation. *He expects you to express a willingness to act the same way toward others.*

Simple unmet needs start to get met because your needs were met. People who are down get encouragement from you. People with a need meet you, and that need gets filled, or you find help to get it filled. You celebrate and honor people who experience a success or victory. The lonely have a new friend. The burdened have a load lifter. The lost have a direction giver. The vulnerable have a protector. Those in pain are comforted. The law of scarcity doesn't apply to you because God's love and supply for you are unlimited. You can afford to be willing. You aren't competing with others any longer, and that frees you to connect with them now. You don't need anything from them. You aren't self-absorbed. You detect needs and are genuinely interested in the well-being of others, even at the expense of your own. God's got you. Those who are close to you see his love at work and feel it in their connection with you. They are receiving the new you and are accepting what you're offering them. They are thanking God. All people who matter to God *now matter to you.*

Deeply loved men deeply love—whatever that means in the moment.

So, chosen by God for this new life of love, dress in the wardrobe God picked out for you: compassion, kindness, humility, quiet strength, discipline. Be even-tempered, content with second place, quick to forgive an offense. Forgive as quickly and completely as the Master forgave you. And regardless of what else you put on, wear love. It's your basic, all-purpose garment. Never be without it.[8]

Chosen by God and secure in him. Other-centered. Imitators of God. Wearing his love. This is the shift God wants.

Let no debt remain outstanding, except the continuing debt to love one another, for whoever loves others has fulfilled the law.[9]

Great Love Shows

Size matters.

The larger the debt that's forgiven, the greater the gratitude, love, and appreciation are *supposed* to be shown toward the Master. The magnitude of the debt is also supposed to be reflected in the magnitude of our personal transformation. We are expected to move from selfish and stingy with grace to compassionate and generous with grace. In both cases, Jesus wants his followers to listen to the stories, project ourselves into them, and assess and personalize our own relationships with him and the people around us. The moneylenders in the different Gospel accounts tracked the actions of those whose debts they forgave. Jesus defines our own encounters with him by tracking how we respond to him and others after we experience his overwhelming love and mercy. The woman who anointed Jesus' feet, represented in his parable of the grateful debtor, became a fearless worshiper of God.

The unmerciful servant, whom the king made whole, remained fearful, self-absorbed, and unfeeling following his encounter with mercy and failed to reproduce it. Overwhelming love and wholeness should overwhelm us—sometimes it does, and sometimes it doesn't. Otherwise, why would Jesus bother drawing the distinction.

In the rooting context and mission of this discussion about God's love, some people have a head-plus-heart (rooted and established) experience with the overwhelming love and security God shows them, and others have a head-minus-heart encounter (established but not rooted). Those who have a head-plus-heart experience emerge rich in their relationships with God and people. Those with a head-minus-heart encounter emerge entitled, poor again, judged, and enslaved. One type of person succeeds and is strengthened in love. The other fails to emotionally grasp the enormity of God's mercy and, instead of soaring in grateful repentance, plateaus with relief. So where is the failure? How can we come out of our own encounters with Jesus possessing much love, much acceptance, much forgiveness, and much wholeness and expressing those experiences the right way?

In our digitally overwhelming, mentally overtaxing, and emotionally draining world, it's hard to see or remember anything for long. Screens are sliding up and down, left and right, and we stare at them all day. Our brains are on overload, and the flood of information, news updates, notifications, TikTok videos, Insta and Facebook posts is unrelenting and unceasing. Perhaps the unmerciful debtor was equally preoccupied with what he perceived he was still missing, because he certainly didn't pause after encountering such great mercy. He immediately went to the place his restless soul said to go. Why? Because he was afraid of losing out on collecting a tiny sliver of debt. In the process, the amazing and overwhelming moment with the king was lost to the next thing, the next nervous twitch, the next restless action. Perhaps we aren't so far removed from this man. I certainly am not. I can get revved up just like the next guy and miss out on amazing moments to stop and stare at God's love for me. I miss intimate moments with Jesus and transformational encounters with others because of all the digital distraction. I have to check myself, and so do you.

Here's why: God's love defines *everything* about those he chooses to love.

All that we are. All that we have. All that we hope, think, dream, desire, and do are designed to be soaked in this special, one-of-a-kind love. It is an overwhelming thing. It is a stopper of men. It demands emotional territory. It calls for pauses every day and makes us vulnerable in its presence. It is selfless, sacrificial, and unconditional. It is unparalleled in scope. It manifests in an ongoing, outgoing, self-sacrificing concern for all people. And here is the most shocking aspect of all: God gives this love without condition and unreservedly to those who are undeserving and inferior to himself. There will never be anything in our lives that can even come close. That is why we need to check our thinking and prioritizing of God's love for us.

It's the kind of love Jesus Christ has for his Father and his followers.

[Jesus prayed,] "Righteous Father, though the world does not know you, I know you, and they know that you have sent me. I have made you known to them, and will continue to make you known in order that the love you have for me may be in them and that I myself may be in them."[10]

Great love authors a great response. Remember the question Jesus asked?

"Now which of them will love him more?"

Simon replied, "I suppose the one who had the bigger debt forgiven."

"You have judged correctly," Jesus said.[11]

Great love was God's choice—in amount, in quality, and in intensity through Christ. God chose to deliver that love, and he has revealed it to you. That was his thoughtful choice within himself. Now you get to choose *within yourself.* What amount will you choose? What quality will you give? With what level of intensity will you love God and others? Will he recognize it? Will you love him more, as he expects, based on his actions toward you? Will you love him the same as other things? Or will you love him less? Will you have the courage to intentionally slow yourself down to know? Will you declare a pause to the noise so you can encounter him? Can you afford to be willing? If you can, he is waiting right now for you to stop:

Stop and see. "What marvelous love the Father has extended to us! Just look at it—we're called children of God! That's who we really are. But that's also why the world doesn't recognize us or take us seriously, because it has no idea who he is or what he's up to. But friends, that's exactly who we are: children of God. And that's only the beginning. Who knows how we'll end up! What we know is that when Christ is openly revealed, we'll see him—and in seeing him, become like him. All of us who look forward to his Coming stay ready, with the glistening purity of Jesus' life as a model for our own."[12]

Stop and wonder why. "It's a wonder God didn't lose his temper and do away with the whole lot of us. Instead, immense in mercy and with an incredible love, he embraced us. He took our sin-dead lives and made us alive in Christ. He did all this on his own, with no help from us! Then he picked us up and set us down in highest heaven in company with Jesus, our Messiah."[13]

Stop and marvel at his mercy. "I was treated mercifully because I didn't know what I was doing—didn't know Who I was doing it against! Grace mixed with faith and love poured over me and into me. And all because of Jesus."[14]

Stop and make a choice. "God's readiness to give and forgive is now public. Salvation's available for everyone! We're being shown how to turn our backs on a godless, indulgent life, and how to take on a God-filled, God-honoring life. This new life is starting right now, and is whetting our appetites for the glorious day when our great God and Savior, Jesus Christ, appears. He offered himself as a sacrifice to free us from a dark, rebellious life into this good, pure life, making us a people he can be proud of, energetic in goodness."[15]

Throw open the doors.

Lord Jesus,

Your love makes me vulnerable. It is so overwhelming and confident toward me. I've never been so deeply loved, and I have trouble taking it all in the way I should and the way you desire. But I'm stopping in this moment you have given me to see, to ponder, to take in, and to marvel at your merciful choice with me. Words don't fit. I was deep in debt to you in every way, and out of your own heart came a choice to forgive, accept, and love me. I see you and what you chose. I see myself as a receiver of your choice, and now I choose. I choose you. I choose now, and forever, to love you back without hesitation or reservation. I choose for the world to see my love for you. I want others to know how grateful I am for what you've done. I want you to know how I feel about you. Your love has made me a forever worshiper. You desire men who are worshipers in spirit and in truth. That is who I want to be. I am throwing open the door. I am standing in pure hope. I am shouting praise. I am committing to living in your love so I can live it out in my life. This is my choice today and forever in faith. Amen.

RESTING SECURE

10

WHEN THE OCEANS RAGE

The Secure Possess Peace in the Midst

MEN ARE LIKE ICEBERGS—only the tip is visible.

Under the waterline of our lives, it gets more human, more unpredictable, and more painful. An older brother commits suicide. Pancreatic cancer takes your mom thirty days after her diagnosis. A second brother succumbs to the suicide lie. Decades of severe mental illness incapacitate, afflict, and consume an entire family's private existence. Federal prison confusingly takes a third brother and personal hero out of your life for five years. Gone. Divorce and family estrangement plague your blood connections. Your wife has multiple miscarriages. Tuition payments for college sit on your chest, creating a quiet and constant desperation. You wonder, *How am I going to do this?* Hard work pays off until it stops paying off, and you plateau for a season. Nothing to show for all your hard work except for a more refined hope. Seriously? Yes, and it gets better in a not-so-good way. You spend decades helping an organization succeed, only to be shown the door. Professional sabotage. Reversals on commitments. Once lofty and noble expectations are delayed. The cavalry doesn't come. The job doesn't come back. The door remains closed. The loss is permanent. And this is just for starters.

Under the waterline of our lives, we see the big pressures and bigger issues no one usually sees. The walk-around pressures and setbacks that rock and confuse us. Life is full of setbacks, but setbacks are not sentences.

All the events I just described happened to me. They *disabled* my spirit but activated my *failsafe*.

failsafe (adjective): Causing a piece of machinery, other mechanism, or person to revert to a safe condition in the event of a breakdown or malfunction.

failsafe (noun): A system or plan or backup that comes into operation in the event of something going wrong or that is there to prevent something from going wrong or poorly. Ex., "the secondary safety system is indeed a failsafe"

Yes, indeed. Thank you, God, that your love was my failsafe every time.

If GOD hadn't been there for me,
    I never would have made it.
The minute I said, "I'm slipping, I'm falling,"
    your love, GOD, took hold and held me fast.

When I was upset and beside myself,
    you calmed me down and cheered me up.[1]

God's unfailing love and faithfulness came through Jesus
Christ.[2]

If you've ever said to yourself, *I don't know how people do life
without Jesus*, God agrees! His love is created to be our failsafe—
our backup system that keeps our thinking and choices from
spiraling in self-destructive or harmful directions. He is our failsafe
in the face of pressures, challenges, and losses. The unplanned and
unwelcome events I mentioned were never part of the script I envi-
sioned for myself. Neither are yours. *By design*, they simply impose
themselves into our stories, testing every conviction, poking every
fear, and magnifying a nagging sense of doubt over everything
discussed in these pages.

Yes, by design. Wait, what?

You may be saying to yourself, *But I've made some bad personal
choices that created equally bad personal consequences.* But think
about it from God's perspective for a moment. Imminent or actual
failure is needed to prove that someone or something in your life is
unfailing. The reality, possibility, or prospect of failure is the context for a failsafe to be activated. When we feel like we're failures.
When we fail to meet the standards we set for ourselves. When
others have failed us. When our physical, emotional, or relational
strength has failed. When we're overwhelmed by the magnitude
of what we're called to do. When all options are exhausted. When
the pain of certain choices feels fatal and final.

God providentially designs moments like these for men who
believe so that we will activate the failsafe of his love by declaring his presence and promise in the middle of the mess and

demonstrating faith by taking some action that acknowledges both. Our spiritual failsafe can then transform a troubling circumstance into a redemptive and purposeful encounter that glorifies God. Mysterious? Of course! God's Spirit is doing his work in our lives, redeeming poor choices, deep injustices, and emotionally confusing situations.

> The Holy Spirit helps us in our weakness. For example, we don't know what God wants us to pray for. But the Holy Spirit prays for us with groanings that cannot be expressed in words. And the Father who knows all hearts knows what the Spirit is saying, for the Spirit pleads for us believers in harmony with God's own will. And we know that God causes everything to work together for the good of those who love God and are called according to his purpose for them.[3]

> Be strong and courageous, and do the work. Don't be afraid or discouraged, for the LORD God, my God, is with you. He will not fail you or forsake you.[4]

King David spoke those "strong and courageous" words to his son (and future king) Solomon around 1000 BC. All this time later, you and I still need this encouragement! This journey of internalizing God's unfailing love and integrating it into the core fabric of our thinking has always been an essential conversation one man must have with another. Like David, I have a prophetic duty as your brother to assure you that you have nothing to fear if God has asked you to do anything to show love for him that you feel may outsize your natural capacities. That's how Solomon felt, and that's how we feel when God is requiring more of us. He also knows that we are limited, and we break down; malfunction; feel insecure, afraid, or anxious; and act out of our pain if we don't have a failsafe to meet the vicissitudes of life head-on. Remember that word: *vicissitudes*. It means "changing or fluctuating circumstances," typically ones that are unwelcome or unpleasant. Jesus said that life was full of vicissitudes. He was honest. But he also declared himself to be our personal failsafe when the vicissitudes of life appear uninvited or unintended.

[Jesus said,] "I have told you [about what will take place] so that you may have peace in me. Here on earth you will have many trials and sorrows. But take heart, because I have overcome the world."[5]

Do you see Jesus' encouragement amid the vicissitudes of life? He said, "Take heart." His peace is an inside thing. Jesus knows things outside us can't resolve the dilemmas within us. How many times did I think that way and miss God's loving purpose. No more! After thousands of personal counseling sessions with men, I can confidently say that the most critical predictive factor for personal fulfillment and success as a man is not circumstantial, financial, or even relational; it is internal and emotional. The inner boy needs to grow up into the inner man who is secure in God's love. This is what God the Father calls *sonship*. The loving sonship we have in Christ is the failsafe solution for when our self-perception becomes unhealthy and we feel insecure. It is our truest identity, and living out our truest identity is when we feel what we long for as men—integrity.

If that feels too therapeutic, touchy-feely, or beyond your world, it's important to note that the main causes of masculine insecurity—pride and fear—are two sides of the same coin. Men are loath to admit they're afraid. Never! But they will confess easily to pride, which is just fear turned inside out. Find prideful actions in any area of a man's life, and I will show you a deeper fear as its source. A prideful man is afraid of losing something—power, control, position, image, acceptance, recognition, or relationship. His fear of losing that thing causes him to compete for what he fears losing out of a false perception of its scarcity. You know what we call that, men?

Pride.

Whether you call it fear or pride, it represents unhealthy and worldly ways of competing for worth. That's why we all want to know—more than anything else—that we matter. More specifically, that who we are is appreciated, and that someone has assigned us value. Find a man who isn't sure about his worth, and I will show you a man who is living out of what he perceives he lacks. He is performing out of a search for permanence and transcendence, no matter how rich or poor, known or unknown, weak or strong, professional or pedestrian he is. It's true of men in every tribe, and it produces broken male culture.

If you don't believe me, simply track the amount of money—billions of dollars—men spend trying to make progress in these matters by seeking out all kinds of digital fantasies. Fantasy risks. Fantasy battles. Fantasy dreams. Fantasy sex. Fantasy conquests. Fantasy sports. Or just fantasy in general. Why pursue fantasy? Because men are fighting to validate their worth, and the world is eager to accommodate them, because it will keep them thirsty and paying. Men living out of what they lack has created billionaires! But no more for you. Now you know and have affirmed both the futility and silliness of that pursuit. You've had the mission-critical conversations with God, yourself, and me about your self-perception and identity, and those conversations must be repeated daily in some form and in community. Everything you hoped or dreamed to get out of life hinges on understanding your worth to God and his love for you, and here's why.

God's ruling is in. And it's final.

GOD told [his people], "I've never quit loving you and
    never will.
  Expect love, love, and more love!"[6]

Stop striving and know that I am God.[7]

The love of God, who is sovereign over the universe, commands rest in a man's spirit. That is why we've journeyed through the basis for that rest, which God wants you to enter in your inner man. This is the revelation that makes men secure, and it's also the revelation that makes Satan insecure. The hater of your soul is always working to dilute what God has proven and promised to you. In fact, using broken male culture, Satan will make you feel that the need for an internal failsafe that secures your self-perception and self-regard is either weak or limited. Why? So that you'll choose his pseudoforms of worth that masquerade as viable sources to meet your inner needs. How do you know these are the devil's cheap imitations? They fail! They fail to meet the deep emotional needs you have. They fail to give you the character you need to do relationships right. They fail to end the restlessness and anxiety you're still experiencing in your soul. They fail to make you more focused on others instead of yourself. They fail to make you generous of spirit and humble of heart. They fail the test of permanence, and you spend more energy chasing after them. It's never enough.

By contrast, Jesus Christ freely offers the only authentic emotional failsafe that secures you permanently and grows a practical responsibility in you! He offers his life to you out of his love and loyalty to you. "Greater love hath no man than this, that a man lay down his life for his friends."[8]

The ultimate act that communicates ultimate worth.

You don't need any other man to tell you.

Jesus did not fail. Your worth is safe.

Head for the Eye

Have you ever needed calm in the midst of a storm? Calm in the chaos?

In October of 2015, the conditions in the waters of the western Pacific Ocean were ripe for a massive tropical cyclone. By the twenty-second of the month, weather forecasters were staring at satellite footage of an impressive tropical cyclone called Champi. While its size was noteworthy, something else caught their attention—*the eye* of the storm! Measuring seventy miles across, the eye of this typhoon was the largest ever recorded.

Scientists and researchers guesstimated that the eye of this storm was so massive that any animal underneath it would be able to take shelter for seven or eight hours before the powerful storm walls hit. The reason for Champi's distinct doughnut shape and big hole in the middle? Large thunderstorms surrounding the eye.

Massive chaos is juxtaposed with powerful peace.

The image of Champi illustrates a profound biblical truth Jesus wants his men to understand. The active, powerful, and pressure-filled experiences Jesus predicted in our lives require a place of rest *in the midst of them*, not in their absence. He said, "I have told you all this so that you may have peace in me"[9] but more often than not, we choose false places of peace that cater to our fears at the expense of our faith. We tell ourselves we can do it and spend our energy attempting to create a storm-free and pain-free existence. We structure our lives to avoid pain. We take precautions. We try to control our environment and interactions. We drive defensively through life. We try to make life as predictable and painless as possible.

By contrast, our sovereign and loving God told us that life would be like a bowling alley. No matter how many times we set and reset the pieces of our lives to ensure order and peace, a bowling ball of brokenness, injustice, or difficulty will eventually come down the lane to knock over some or all of our carefully placed pieces. We're helpless to stop them, and while we may feel alone, we're not. In fact, according to Jesus, we aren't called to stop the storms of life from bowling us over. We're supposed to head for the eye of the storm—the place of peace in the midst of the chaos.

> As evening came, Jesus said to his disciples, "Let's cross to the other side of the lake." So they took Jesus in the boat and started out, leaving the crowds behind (although other boats followed). But soon a fierce storm came up. High waves were breaking into the boat, and it began to fill with water.
>
> Jesus was sleeping at the back of the boat with his head on a cushion. The disciples woke him up, shouting, "Teacher, don't you care that we're going to drown?"
>
> When Jesus woke up, he rebuked the wind and said to the waves, "Silence! Be still!" Suddenly the wind stopped, and there was a great calm. Then he asked them, "Why are you afraid? Do you still have no faith?"[10]

Jesus didn't say, "Man, those waves hitting the boat are massive!" Instead, he asked, "Why are you afraid? Do you still have no faith?" Why did he respond this way? Not because the storm disturbed him, but because the disciples' lack of faith disturbed him. He was with them in the boat, but they let fear take over. What the disciples chose to *do* with their fear made all the difference to

Jesus. It was personal to him. So what did they do with their fear to get such a response from Christ?

They accused Jesus of *not caring*.

Make no mistake, a small boat in the midst of a huge storm is a scary place to be, so the disciples' initial fear response wasn't wrong. God isn't asking us not to fear in the face of overwhelming circumstances or challenges or potential losses. That's human. But when we think that Jesus doesn't care about us or love us in the midst of our storms, our faith in God's full acceptance and love has been replaced by fear. Sometimes it may feel as if God is sleeping in the midst of the storms of our lives, and it takes a lot of faith in a "sleeping" God to know and rely on his love for us.

In faith, we head for the eye of the storm—the place of God's caring and calming love.

> We who have run for our very lives to God have every
> reason to grab the promised hope with both hands and
> never let go. It's an unbreakable spiritual lifeline, reaching
> past all appearances right to the very presence of God
> where Jesus, running on ahead of us, has taken up his
> permanent post as high priest for us.[11]

We run for the "eye" of God's love to rest secure.

Because I Know That You Love Me

My friends Derek Johnson and Chris Quilala of the band Jesus Culture wrote a song called "Your Love Never Fails" that sums up our journey into God's love so well. While I'm not the best singer, I do love declaring in faith this part of the song because it activates the failsafe of God's love in my life *in the midst* of my daily battles to remain in his love as Jesus commanded.

When the oceans rage
I don't have to be afraid
Because I know that you love me
Your love never fails

The wind is strong and the water's deep
I'm not alone in these open seas
'Cause Your love never fails

The chasm is far too wide
I never thought I'd reach the other side
'Cause Your love never fails

When I know, with my head and my heart, that God loves me in the middle of my adversities, I am free. He can't fail me. He's lovingly working out his plans for my life. This means I am free to forget about myself—not to think less of myself but to think of myself less. That's a good sign of inner security I'm working on every day. I am also free not to care about what people think so much. While I'm always going to care on some level, I no longer have anything to prove to anyone—even myself. God sets my standard worth, not people and, for sure, not me. That dominoes into the next space of freedom that is even more wonderful for an active Christian: I can now do things for the joy of doing them. I can help people to help people, not to feel better about myself or to flood my social media. It's the overflow of being reminded of and being filled with the knowledge of God's love in the moment. It's an amazing and counterintuitive thing to not care what people think but to make yourself available to all people. All I know is it sure feels good, and it's another sign that I'm growing in God's love.

Though I am free and belong to no one, I have made myself a slave to everyone, to win as many as possible.[12]

Because I know that he loves me.

I feel like I'm singing out with my life God's ultimate verdict about me. It's taken a while, but I can see I'm starting to believe it because my behaviors reflect it. And that is my prayer for you. A man connected to the truth of God's love in your *inner man* such that your *outer man* reflects that you have accepted God's acceptance of you.

Please hear me one final time: *Your worth is not on trial anymore.* Say it out loud, because God has declared it. Tell yourself what God has spoken through Christ. Speak it. Grasp this truest truth about yourself like a life vest in a raging ocean, and never let a lie wrench it away from your spirit.

As we wind down this journey of illuminating and internalizing God's love, let's complete our faith in it with an action expressing our desire.

Receive this blessing from me to you:

[I] get down on my knees before the Father, this magnificent Father who parcels out all heaven and earth. I ask him to strengthen you by his Spirit—not a brute strength but a glorious inner strength—that Christ will live in you as you open the door and invite him in. And I ask him that with both feet planted firmly on love, you'll be able to take in with all followers of Jesus the extravagant dimensions of Christ's love. Reach out and experience the breadth! Test its length! Plumb the depths! Rise to the heights! Live full lives, full in the fullness of God.[13]

Amen.

NOTES

INTRODUCTION: THE INNER MAN
1. John 15:19.
2. Blaise Pascal, *Pensées* (New York: Penguin Books, 1995), 45.
3. See, for example, Romans 7:22, 2 Corinthians 4:16, and Ephesians 3:16 in the NASB (1995).
4. Ephesians 3:14-19, NASB (1995).
5. Zephaniah 3:17.
6. Matthew 15:8.
7. Romans 8:31-37.
8. 2 Corinthians 5:14, NASB.
9. John 15:9.

1: THE FIGHT IS OVER
1. Jeremiah 29:12-14.
2. Acts 15:8-11.
3. Matthew 3:16-17.
4. See Romans 8:31-37.
5. Mark 12:14.
6. Erin Brodwin, "Why Ebola Is Such a Uniquely Terrible Virus," *Business Insider*, October 15, 2014, http://www.businessinsider.com/what-makes -ebola-virus-so-deadly-2014-10.
7. Proverbs 29:25-26.
8. John 12:42-43.
9. Luke 22:24-26.

10. Galatians 5:13-15.
11. Jeremiah 3:19.
12. Matthew 6:8-9.
13. Romans 8:15-16.
14. John 8:29.
15. Romans 8:37.
16. 1 John 4:18.
17. 2 Timothy 1:7.
18. Matthew 3:17.

2: YOU WOULD DO THAT FOR ME?

1. David Stubbings, "A Timeline of the Biggest Waves Surfed as Rodrigo Koxa Sets New Record," Guinness World Records, May 1, 2018, https://www.guinnessworldrecords.com/news/2018/5/a-timeline-of-the-biggest-waves-surfed-as-rodrigo-koxa-sets-new-record-523752?fb_comment_id=1668905369890995_1677312895716909.
2. "Japanese Sushi Tycoon Pays Record Tuna Price," BBC News, January 5, 2019, https://www.bbc.com/news/world-asia-46767370#:~:text=A%20Japanese%20sushi%20boss%20has,which%20he%20paid%20in%202013.
3. John 13:1-5, NLT.
4. John 10:11.
5. Matthew 26:39.
6. 2 Corinthians 5:14-15.
7. Romans 8:31-35, 37-39, MSG.
8. Ephesians 3:17-19.
9. John 16:33.
10. Matthew 10:29-30.
11. Psalm 84:2-4.
12. Psalm 40:1.
13. Romans 8:37.
14. 1 Peter 1:6-9, MSG.

3: SOMEONE HAS TO DIE

1. Ecclesiastes 2:11, MSG.
2. Mark 8:34-35.
3. Romans 6:8-11, NASB.
4. Weekend at Bernie's, directed by Ted Kotcheff (Los Angeles: Twentieth Century Fox, 1989).
5. Mark 4:35, NASB.
6. Psalm 40:2.

7. Matthew 22:16.
8. Matthew 3:17.
9. Ephesians 3:18-19.
10. Galatians 2:20.
11. Romans 6:6-7.
12. Colossians 3:5-10.
13. Romans 6:4-5, 10-13.
14. Ephesians 2:4-5.
15. Ephesians 2:6-7.
16. Colossians 3:1-4.
17. Ephesians 2:18-19.
18. Hebrews 4:16.
19. Philippians 3:7-12, NLT.
20. Hebrews 11:6, MSG.

4: FIERCELY COMFORTABLE

1. 1 Corinthians 13:11.
2. Ephesians 3:16-17, NASB (1995), emphasis added.
3. Ephesians 4:12-16, MSG.
4. Romans 8:28-29.
5. Philippians 2:1-2.
6. John 8:36.
7. Galatians 5:19-23, MSG.
8. 2 Corinthians 5:17-18, MSG.
9. See Genesis 50:20.
10. Matthew 11:28-29.
11. See Matthew 12:35.
12. Philippians 1:6, MSG.
13. Romans 7:24–8:2, MSG.

5: SECURITY THREATS

1. "The Total Number of Records Exposed in 2019 Has Hit 15.1 Billion, an Increase of 284% on the Previous Year, as the Number of Breaches Reaches an All-Time High," Benzinga, February 12, 2020, https://www.benzinga.com/pressreleases/20/02/p15318330/the-total-number-of-records-exposed-in-2019-has-hit-15-1-billion-an-increase-of-284-on-the-previou#:~:text=February%2012%2C%202020-,Risk%20Based%20Security%20today%20released%20their%202019%20Year%20End%20Data,records%20exposed%20shattering%20industry%20projections.
2. "First Three Quarters of 2019: 7.2 Billion Malware Attacks, 151.9

Million Ransomware Attacks," Security Magazine, October 22, 2019, https://www.securitymagazine.com/articles/91133-first-three-quarters -of-2019-72-billion-malware-attacks-1519-million-ransomware -attacks#:~:text=Million%20Ransomware%20Attacks-,First%20Three %20Quarters%20of%202019%3A%207.2%20Billion,Attacks%2C %20151.9%20Million%20Ransomware%20Attacks&text=In%20the %20first%20three%20quarters,over%2Dyear%20declines%2C %20respectively.

3. Proverbs 14:12, NASB.

4. Psalm 15:4, KJV.

5. Psalm 143:8.

6. Matthew 22:37.

7. Luke 1:46-48.

8. Judges 3:7.

9. Isaiah 26:3, NLT.

10. Psalm 118:24, NASB.

11. Lamentations 3:21-23.

12. C. S. Lewis, *Mere Christianity* (New York: Macmillan, 1952; repr., Westwood, NJ: Barbour), 40.

13. 2 Corinthians 10:3-6, MSG.

14. Psalm 37:30-31, NASB.

15. Matthew 4:10, NASB.

16. Psalm 118:24, NLT.

17. Colossians 3:1-2, MSG.

18. Proverbs 27:19, NCV.

19. Mark 12:30, NCV.

6: THE HEAD AND THE HEART

1. Matthew 15:8.

2. Jeremiah 31:3, MSG.

3. Romans 5:5.

4. Ephesians 3:17-19.

5. 1 Peter 1:8.

6. Joel C. Rosenberg, "Coronavirus Pandemic Is a Wake Up Call: Exclusive Joshua Fund Poll," Joshua Fund, March 2020, https:// www.joshuafund.com/learn/news-article/coronavirus_pandemic _is_a_wake_up_call_exclusive_joshua_fund_poll.

7. John 4:10-11.

8. John 7:37-38.

9. John 3:16.

10. Isaiah 57:14.
11. 2 Corinthians 10:4, NLT.
12. 2 Corinthians 10:4-5, NLT.
13. Matthew 4:3-4, NLT.
14. James 1:22-25, MSG.
15. 1 John 4:16-17.
16. John 16:27.
17. John 15:9-11.
18. John 13:34-35.
19. Romans 13:8-9.

7: EACH DAY

1. Matthew 12:33, 35.
2. Isaiah 5:7, NLT.
3. John 15:1-2, 6.
4. Colossians 2:6-7, NLT.
5. Philippians 1:6, MSG.
6. Jeremiah 17:7-8.
7. Ezekiel 31:4-7.
8. 2 Peter 1:5-8.
9. Matthew 7:24-27, MSG.
10. John 16:13-15.
11. John 14:6.
12. John 3:19-21, MSG.
13. John 7:18.
14. 1 Thessalonians 5:16-18, MSG.
15. Psalm 118:24, NASB.
16. Psalm 119:71, NASB.
17. Ecclesiastes 3:11, NLT.
18. Hebrews 13:15, NLT.
19. Psalm 23:4-6, NLT.
20. Matthew 11:28-30, MSG.
21. 1 Kings 19:12, KJV.
22. Isaiah 41:10, MSG.
23. Romans 8:38-39, MSG.
24. Isaiah 43:18-19.

8: SHOCK AND AWESOME

1. Hebrews 11:1.
2. Hebrews 10:38-39.
3. Jeremiah 9:23-24, MSG.

4. 1 Timothy 6:11-12.
5. Luke 22:42.
6. Romans 12:1, NLT.
7. Matthew 16:18-19.
8. Matthew 6:9-10.
9. Matthew 5:10-12.
10. Luke 4:18-19, MSG.
11. Matthew 11:18-19.
12. Romans 4:18-24.

9: THROWING OPEN THE DOORS

1. Luke 7:36-39.
2. Luke 7:40-47.
3. Romans 5:1-2, MSG.
4. Philippians 3:7-9, MSG.
5. Matthew 18:23-27, NASB.
6. Matthew 18:28-30, NASB.
7. Matthew 18:31-35, NASB.
8. Colossians 3:12-14, MSG.
9. Romans 13:8.
10. John 17:25-26.
11. Luke 7:42-43.
12. 1 John 3:1-3, MSG.
13. Ephesians 2:3-6, MSG.
14. 1 Timothy 1:13-14, MSG.
15. Titus 2:11-14, MSG.

10: WHEN THE OCEANS RAGE

1. Psalm 94:17-19, MSG.
2. John 1:17, NLT.
3. Romans 8:26-28, NLT.
4. 1 Chronicles 28:20, NLT.
5. John 16:33, NLT.
6. Jeremiah 31:3, MSG.
7. Psalm 46:10, NASB.
8. John 15:13, KJV.
9. John 16:33, NLT.
10. Mark 4:35-40, NLT.
11. Hebrews 6:18-20, MSG.
12. 1 Corinthians 9:19.
13. Ephesians 3:14-19, MSG.